Roaming Kyrgyzstan

Beyond The Tourist Track

JESSICA JACOBSON

iUniverse, Inc.
New York   Bloomington

Roaming Kyrgyzstan
Beyond the Tourist Track

iUniverse books may be ordered through booksellers or by contacting:

iUniverse
1663 Liberty Drive
Bloomington, IN 47403
www.iuniverse.com
1-800-Authors (1-800-288-4677)

ISBN: 978-0-595-52686-4 (pbk)
ISBN: 978-0-595-62740-0 (ebk)

Printed in the United States of America

Contents

INTRODUCTION   I

ACKNOWLEDGEMENTS   I

HISTORY   4

TRAVEL ESSENTIALS   7

VISAS   8

AIR TRAVEL   8

TRAIN TRAVEL   9

TIME   10

ELECTRICITY   10

LANGUAGES   10

LOCATION   10

WEATHER   10

WATER   10

SAFETY   10

CURRENCY   10

HEALTH   11

EMBASSIES   11

VEHICLE TRAVEL   12

WHAT TO BRING   12

COMMUNICATIONS   12

FOOD   13

TRADITIONS   15

WORDS YOU MAY HEAR   17

NATIONAL HOLIDAYS   17

EVENTS   18

PUBLICATIONS   18

Non-fiction books   18

Guidebooks   19

Fiction books   19

Media   20

Films: 20

Web sites   21

CHUI REGION   23

BISHKEK   24

Where to Sleep   24

Where to Eat   28

The People of Kyrgyzstan – Bishkek Shopkeeper   37

What to Do   39

Theater   40

Nightlife 44
Transport 45
In town: 45
Reliable drivers: 46
Out of Bishkek: 46
Other Services 48
The Places of Kyrgyzstan – Bishkek 50
Community Based Tourism 56
The Traditions of Kyrgyzstan – Nooruz 58
Excursions from Bishkek 60
THE PLACES OF KYRGYZSTAN – ISSYK-ATA 62

TOKMOK AREA 69
TOKMOK 70

KARABALTA AREA 71
KARAKUL 72
TASH-KUMYR 72

ISSYK-KUL REGION 73
BALIKCHY 75
Where to Sleep 75
Where to Eat 75
Transportation 75
TAMCHY 76
Where to Sleep 76
Where to Eat 76
What to Do 77
Transportation 77
Other Services 77
CHOK-TAL 77
CHOLPON-ATA 78
Where to Sleep 78
Where to Eat 78
What to Do 78
Transportation 79
Other Services 79
BOSTERI 79
Where to Sleep 79
Where to Eat 81
What to Do 81
Transportation 81
Other Services 81
KOMSOMOL 82

KARAGAI-BULAK   82
GRIGOREVKA   82
SEMYONOVKA   83
ANANYEVO   84
   Where to Sleep   84
   Where to Eat   84
   What to Do   84
   Transportation   85
KUTURGU   85
ADDITIONAL LODGING OPTIONS IN NORTHERN ISSYK-KUL   85
   Intimak (Tyup region)   85
   Karagai-Bulak   85
   Korumdu   85
   Bulan-Sogotu   86
   Bosteri   86
   Kara-Oi   87
   Chon-Sari-Oi   87
   Kara Choi Oy   87
   Kosh-Kol   88
   Toru-Aigyr   88

TYUP REGION   89
TYUP   90
   Where to Sleep   90

AK-SUU REGION   91
KARAKOL   92
   Where to Sleep   92
   Where to Eat   94
   What to Do   94
   The Places of Kyrgyzstan – Karakol   96
   Transportation   98
   Other Services   99
AK-SUU   100
JETI-OGUZ   100
   Where to Sleep   101
   Where to eat   101
   Transportation   102
   What to Do   102
THE SOUTH SHORE (BETWEEN JETI-OGUZ AND BARSKOON)   103
BARSKOON   105
TAMGA   105
   Where to Sleep   105

Transportation 106
What to Do 106

TON REGION 107

Tosor 108
**Khaji-Say 108
Ton 109
Bokonbaevo 109
Where to Sleep 109
Where to eat 110
Transportation 110
Other services 110
Kara-Koo 112
Ortuk 113

NARYN REGION 115

Kochkor 116
Where to Sleep 116
Where to Eat 116
What to Do 116
Transportation 116
Other Services 117
Tuz 117
Near Tuz 118
Son-Kul 118
Where to Sleep 119
Where to Eat 119
What to Do 119
Transportation 119
The Places of Kyrgyzstan – Son-Kul 120
Naryn 122
Where to Sleep 122
Where to Eat 122
What to Do 123
Transportation 123
The People of Kyrgyzstan – Naryn Taxi Driver 124
Other Services 126
Excursions from Naryn 126
**Tash Rabat 127
The Places of Kyrgyzstan – Lake on the Roof 128
Crossing into China 131

TALAS REGION 133

Talas 134

Where to Sleep   134
The Places of Kyrgyzstan – Talas   136
Where to Eat   137
What to Do   138
Transportation   138
Other Services   139
Near Talas   140
**SHEKER   143
What to Do   143
Transportation   144
**KOK SAI   144
Where to Stay   144
What to Do   144
Transportation   145
KIROVKA (KYZYL-ADIR)   145
Transportation   146
SARY-CHELEK BIOSPHERE RESERVE   147
Where to Sleep   148
Where to Eat   148
What to Do   148
Transportation   148

JALAL-ABAD REGION   149
JALALABAT   150
Where to Sleep   150
Where to Eat   151
What to Do   152
THE TRADITIONS OF KYRGYZSTAN – KHURBAN-EID   153
Transportation   156
Other Services   156
**ARSALANBOB   157
Where to Sleep   157
WHAT TO DO   158
Transportation   159

OSH REGION   161
OSH   163
Where to Sleep   164
THE PLACES OF KYRGYZSTAN – OSH   166
Where to Eat   167
THE TRADITIONS OF KYRGYZSTAN – *CHAIKHANA*   170
What to Do   174
Transportation   177

Other Services 178
THE PEOPLE OF KYRGYZSTAN – A STOLEN BRIDE 180
KARA-SUU 184
Where to Eat 184
Transportation 185
**KARAGOI 185
UZGEN 185
Where to Sleep 186
Where to Eat 186
What to Do 186
Transportation 187
THE PLACES OF KYRGYZSTAN – UZGEN 188
KURSHAB 189
ARAVAN 189
KARA-SHORO NATIONAL PARK 189
Where to Sleep 190
Where to Eat 190
POPAN 190
NOOKAT 190
Where to Sleep 190
Where to Eat 191
What to Do 191
Transportation 191
ABSHIR-ATA 192
KYZYL-KIA 192
Where to Stay 192
Where to Eat 193
What to Do 193
Transportation 193
Other Services 193
KOJO-KELEN 193
BATKEN 194
GULCHA 195
SARY-MOGUL 195
CROSSING INTO CHINA 195
CROSSING INTO TAJIKISTAN 196
CROSSING INTO KAZAKHSTAN 196
INDEX 199

Introduction

This book was written during the course of two and half years living, working and traveling throughout Kyrgyzstan. During my time there, I discovered a magical country populated by diverse and hospitable people. My goal in this book is to introduce travelers to the people and cultures of Kyrgyzstan.

In addition to comprehensive information about the best places to stay, eat, and visit, this book includes a series of vignettes from my experiences in Kyrgyzstan. These vignettes are intended to bring the place and the people to life in a way that a standard overview can't accomplish. In order to protect their privacy, the names and identifying details of some individuals mentioned in the vignettes have been changed.

The prices listed were accurate at the time of research. They can be expected to fluctuate, especially transportation and services in the popular tourist destinations, such as Issyk-Kul.

Items marked with a double asterisk (**) are especially recommended by the author. Please send comments, feedback and questions to: jesjacobson@gmail.com and keep up with the author's current travels at http://jjstravels.blogspot.com/.

Wishing you a wonderful journey to Kyrgyzstan.

Acknowledgements

Special thanks go to Guliza Shatmanova, James Reisman, Durusbek Sadikov, Joe and Caroline McDonald, Dmitriy, Asylbek Rajiev, members of the Internet Writing Workshop (especially Rich Maffeo, June Gallant, Gary Presley, Sarah Morgan, Ellen Dreyer and Kathy Highcove), Guliya Raeva, Valery Serebrennikov, Aijamal, Eugene Imas, Courtney Calvin, Charlotte Cooper, Sage Cohen, Aleksey Paniklov, Cale Wagner, Kyle Flanders, Larry Tweed, Kris Rees, Ainura Adylbekova, Karen Gardinier, Vika Safina, Tanja Maiwald, Natalia Fefilova, Mark McEuen, Azamat Baltabaev, Salima Sadikova, Habib, Farhad, Faruh and Lutfulo Jumabeav and all the kind and hospitable citizens of Kyrgyzstan, too numerous to mention, who shared their country and their culture with me.

Kyrgyzstan is a nature-lover's dream. With 50% of the land covered by mountains and 94% of the country above 1000 meters (3,280 feet), the population of 5 million is concentrated in the lowlands, leaving plenty of wild territory for herders, hikers and explorers. These mountains include some of the world's tallest peaks - Peak Pobeda or Jengish Chokosu (7439 meters or 24,406 feet), Peak Lenin (7134 meters or 23, 405 feet) and Khan-Tengri (6995 meters or 22,949 feet). The mighty Tien Shan, stretch 2,800 kilometers (1740 miles) from Tashkent, Uzbekistan, across Kyrgyzstan and into China. About 40,000 streams and rivers gush through the mountain landscape, including the powerful Naryn River, which crosses most of the country before flowing into the Syr Darya on its way to the Aral Sea. Almost 2000 mountain lakes can be found nestled among the peaks.

Kyrgyzstan is also especially attractive to those interested in culture. The country is a mixture of ethnicities (67% Kyrgyz, 14% Uzbek, 11% Russian, and 8% Dungan, Uighur and other) and religions (75% Muslim, 20% Russian Orthodox and 5% other). The especially friendly population offers a unique look into the local life and culture, as well as traditional practices, such as raising lifestock on a *jailoo*, making traditional felt carpets or *shyrdaks* or hunting with golden eagles.

The height of the tourist season extends from June through September, when high altitude climbing, horseback riding and visits to a *jailoo* can all be accomplished. Summer is also the best time to visit Lake Issyk-Kul. The winter months bring less crowds and the best-value skiing in the region at Kyrgyzstan's fledging ski bases.

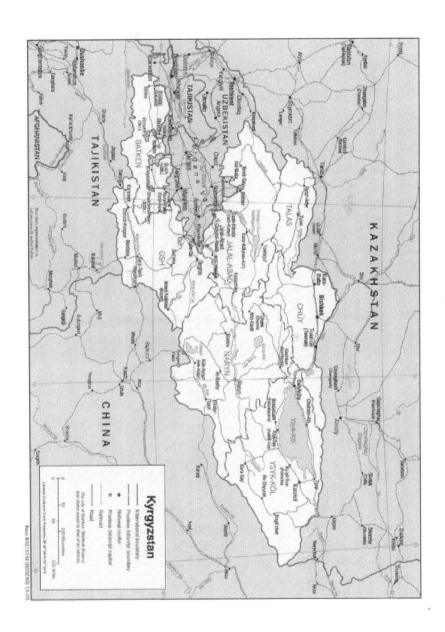

History

The Kyrgyz people appeared in written records (Sima Qian's Records of the Grand Historian) over 2,000 years ago. They lived in the Yenisey River valley of central Siberia. They are described by Muslim and Chinese sources of the 7th to 12th century as being fair with red hair and green or blue eyes. Recently, the Kyrgyz descent from indigenous Siberians has been confirmed by DNA.

In 840 the Kyrgyz revolted against the Uighur Kaganate and with their gain in power, expanded to the Tien Shan region. By the twelfth century though, the Mongol expansion had limited Kyrgyz influence to the Altai and the Sayan Mountains. As the Mongol influence grew, then Russians expanded east, the Kyrgyz moved south.

A series of Turkic peoples ruled over the Kyrgyz until 1685, when the Oirats assumed control. The Kyrgyz tribes achieved freedom in 1510, but then proceeded to be beholden to first the Kalmyks then the Manchus and in the early nineteenth century, the Uzbeks.

The Khanate of Khokand controlled the southern part of Kyrgyzstan in the early 1800s. But in 1876 the Russian Empire occupied and formally annexed it. Many revolts against tsarist authority ensued, with some Kyrgyz moving to Afghanistan or the Pamir Mountains. The most substantial rebellion, inspired by the Russian imposition of the military draft on the Kyrgyz, took place in 1916 and was brutally repressed. This caused many Kyrgyz to escape to China.

Soviet rule began in Kyrgyz territory in 1918. In 1924 the Kara-Kyrgyz Autonomous Oblast was formed, later renamed the Kirghiz Autonomous Soviet Socialist Republic. In 1936 the Kirghiz Soviet Socialist Republic became a full union republic of the Soviet Union.

The Kyrgyz were able to retain many aspects of their traditional culture, despite repression of nationalism. In October 1991, Askar Akayev became the first president of independent Kyrgyzstan, running unopposed. Corruption scandals appeared within his first years in office, however he was reelected again in 1995, running against two candidates. Two rounds of Parliamentary elections in 2000 were determined by the OSCE to be invalid. Elections held in 2005 were deemed an improvement from 2000 but still didn't comply with commitments to fair and free elections. Protestors reacting to fraud in these elections staged a series of meetings that culminated in calls for the government to resign. Much of the counry was surprised when a massive protest in Bishkek (initiated by residents from the south of the country) seized the main government building and President Akayev fled.

Kurmanbek Bakiyev, the former prime minister under Akayev (2000-2002) and the leader of the People's Movement of Kyrgyzstan, was appointed acting President by the Legislative Assembly on March 24, 2005. On July 10, 2005 Bakiyev won the Presidential election with a 53% turnout and 89% of the vote. With Bakiyev garnering much of his support from the south, he inspired hope among southerners that their region would receive more attention from the federal government.

In 2006, large protests against Bakiyev took place. Protesters claimed that Bakiyev didn't honor his promises to limit presidential power, to increase the power of the prime minister and the parliament and to reduce crime and corruption. Another series of large protests occurred in April 2007, demanding Bakiyev's resignation. On April 10 Bakiyev signed constitutional amendments to reduce his own power, but the protests continued until April 19th, when they ended after clashes with police.

TRAVEL ESSENTIALS

Visas

For complete visa requirements, check the website of the Ministry of Foreign Affairs of the Kyrgyz Republic (http://www.mfa.kg/). Most travelers can buy a one month, single entry visa on arrival at Manas airport for $36 or a double entry for $56. Transit visas cost $21 for up to five days, $36 for double entry.

Upon arrival, go to the doorway on the far left. Don't make the mistake of waiting in one of the passport/visa inspection lines. Obtaining the visa takes only minutes. You'll then stand in the passport/visa inspection line along with the others.

Visas can't be obtained at land crossings, and given the very early morning arrivals of all international flights, you might be grateful if you've gotten your visa ahead of time.

Citizens of Azerbaijan, Armenia, Georgia, Moldova, Belarus, Kazakhstan, Russia, Tajikistan, Albania, Bulgaria, Bosnia, Vietnam, Cuba, Macedonia, Poland, Romania, Serbia, Slovakia, Slovenia, Czech Republic, Malaysia, Turkey, Croatia, North Korea, Ukraine and Mongolia can enter Kyrgyzstan without a visa.

The Caucasus and Central Asia

Air travel

Aeroflot, Altyn Air, British Air, China Xinjiang Airlines, Kyrgyzstan Airlines, Turkish Air and Uzbek Air service Bishkek. Additionally, KLM and Lufthansa service Almaty, 250 kilometers (155 miles) to the north. However, to fly into Kyrgyzstan through Almaty, you will need both Kyrgyz and Kazakh visas.

Manas International Airport (Tel: 693109; info@airport.kg; http://www.airport.kg/eng/index.html) is located 30-40 minutes from central Bishkek. There are **exchange booths** on the first and second floor of the airport, offering slightly lower rates than what is available in town. The second floor booth is open early.

There is a **$10 departure tax** for international flights. You pay it at the *kassa* before checking in for your flight.

Almost all international flights arrive and leave in the middle of the night, 3-6 a.m. being the most popular time.

After picking up your baggage, foreigners will need to fill out a **small white information card**. It's quick and simple, asking about your nationality, age and purpose of visit. Hand it to the customs agent on your way out.

In the domestic terminal, there is a left luggage area, a 24-hour café, post office, shop and pharmacy.

You can fly to Bishkek from London (British Air, 9 hours), Istanbul (Turkish Air, 6 hours), Urumqi (Itek Air, 2 hours) and Moscow (Aeroflot, Altyn Air, 4.5 hours). Flights to Almaty include British Air from London, Lufthansa from Frankfurt and KLM from Amsterdam. British Air (Tel: 664220; Open Mon, Thu, Sat 10:30-4; Tues, Fri, Sun 3:30-8 a.m.) has a reputation for frequently misplacing luggage enroute. Luggage is occasionally opened and rifled through (and sealed letters opened) at the Moscow airport.

Local airlines Air Traffic, Kyrgyzstan and Essen Air fly regularly to Osh and Jalal-Abad. For updated schedules, check http://eng.concept.kg/OshConcept/schedule.

If you have a Kazazh visa, the Almaty airport can be a good arrival or departure alternative to Bishkek. Several airlines, including KLM (Tel in Almaty: (0073272) 507747 and Lufthansa offer free bus service between Bishkek and the Almaty airport). The KLM bus charges 100 som per passenger on the Bishkek-Almaty leg for customs.

A cheap way to fly in to Kyrgyzstan is on Pulkovo Airlines, a Russian company that uses Tupolevs. Flights go from several European cities through St. Petersburg to Bishkek.

To take a cab from the airport, stop at one of the taxi cab offices on your way out. You'll pay there and the company will provide a slip to your driver.

Train Travel

There are 3 trains to Russia per week – two Russian (better quality) and one Kyrygz. The trip to Moscow takes 4 days over 3700 kilometers (2300 miles) and costs about 5000 som.

Time

5 hours ahead of GMT.

Electricity

220 volt, 50 hz.

Languages

Kyrgyz and Russian are the official languages. Uzbek is prevalent in the south. Many in Bishkek speak English.

Location

Kyrgyzstan is 198,500 square kilometers (76,600 square miles). It borders Uzbekistan, Kazakhstan, China, and Tajikistan.

Weather

The average temperature in January ranges from -40 to 25 degrees Fahrenheit. In July it ranges from 54 to 104 degrees. Naryn, Karakol and the mountain areas tend to be the coldest areas, Balikchy is known for frequent strong winds and the south of the country has a warmer climate than the north.

Water

Tapwater in the major cities is usually potable, but bottled water is available. Kyrgyzstan has many natural mineral springs in the mountains. If you pass one, they are good places to fill up water bottles.

Safety

Emergency numbers include: police (102), ambulance (103), fire (101), rescue (161) and accidents (530181 in Bishkek, 0312 630900 or 630901 outside Bishkek). Generally, Kyrgyzstan is a very safe place.

Currency

The Kyrgyz Som. The exchange rate is approximately 36 som to the U.S. dollar, 57 som to the Euro. Most transactions take place in cash, though western-oriented restaurants, supermarkets and hotels now accept credit cards. Vendors will occasionally accept dollars or euros. Outside of Bishkek, Osh, Jalalabat and Issyk-Kul, it is best to arrive with the som you'll need.

Health

For quality medical care in Bishkek, try **OnClinic** (ul. Lva Tolstovo 110; Tel: 653131; www.onclinic.kg) or **Neomed** (ul. Gorkovo 21; Tel./Fax: 906090; neomed@neomed.kg; www.neomed.kg). You can also try the **German-Kyrgyz Medical Center** (on ul. Ahunbaeva 92 and Zhukaeva Pudovkina, near the Phys Culture Institute and the Inst. Of Oncologoy; Tel: 512197; 540555; Fax: 540747). They are open until 5 p.m. and take 300 som for a consultation. Prices could be contentious though, as the official price list for foreigners is quite high, quoting $30-60 for consultations and $200 for a medical exam in the hospital.

Dental Clinic **Meerim** (Dr. Stanislav, Dr. Bahtygul or Dr. Aibek) is the clinic used by the Peace Corps. It's located on 144A ulitsa Bokonbaevo, between Logvinenko and Togolok Moldo; Tel: 664069. Open Monday-Friday 8-4.

Dental clinic **Hollywood Smile** (ul. Kievskaya 112; Tel: 666522) is often used by foreigners.

There are drug stores all throughout town. Look for **aptieka** signs. For colds, locals recommend the medicines Coldrex or Fevrex, available from pharmacies.

Embassies

Canada (consulate) – ul. Moskovskaya 189; Tel: 650506, Fax: 650101

China – ul. Toktogula 196; Tel: 212573, 222423

France – ul. Razzakova 49; Tel: 660053

Germany – ul. Razzakova 28; Tel: 666624; Fax: 666636

Great Britian – (in Almaty); Tel: 7 (3272) 506191

India – 164 Chui Prospect; Tel: 210863, 210862, Fax: 660708

Iran - ul. Razzakova 36; Tel: 227214, 226964

Italy – Tel: 690051

Kazakhstan – ul. Togolok Moldo 10; Tel: 660164, 660415

Pakistan – ul. Panfilova 347a; Tel: 227209, 621699

Russia: ul. Razzakova 17; Tel: 624736

Switzerland: ul. Panfilova 144; Tel: 666480; Fax: 664489

Tajikistan: ul. Kara-Darynskaya 36; Kok-Jar microrayon; Tel: 511464

USA – 171 Manas Prospect; Tel: 551243, 551241; Fax: 551264

Turkey – ul. Moskovskaya 89; Tel: 622354, 620378; Fax: 622364
Uzbekistan: ul. Tynystanova 213; Tel: 226171, 662065

Vehicle travel

Most travel within the country is done by *marshrutkis* (mini passenger buses) and shared taxis. In a shared taxi, you pay for one of four spaces. If you want the entire car, pay the per person rate times four. If you want to be picked up at your door, either call an official taxi company (in Bishkek or Osh – this option is more expensive) or stop by the station where the shared taxis depart and you can arrange to have one pick you up. Both types of taxis are safe and reliable. The only variable is the alertness, skill and speed of the driver. Ask around for drivers others recommend. When you find one you like, take his number. Drivers appreciate an advance order by phone, instead of having to wait for passengers at the station.

Allianz and Deniz oil are the two gas stations most trusted for the quality of gas. Others can vary in price and quality.

What to Bring

Almost everything you could want is available now in Bishkek. Bring any clothes you can't live without, any special sports equipment, and small gifts from your place of origin for your hosts and friends you make along the way.

Communications

The country code is 996. International calls can be made cheaply at many internet cafes with ip-telephony services, or from telephone offices attached to post offices. Bishkek phone numbers have 6 digits, Osh numbers have 5.

People like to joke about the Kyrgyz postal system, but everything I sent got to its destination and I received everything I expected. Letters take about nine days from and two weeks to the States from Bishkek. The **central post office** is located at 96 Chui (Tel: 626045, 662561; open Mon-Sat 7-8, Sun and holidays 8-7) and sells postage, cards, newspaper and internet access.

Dial 160 to find out telephone codes

Dial 109 for information

The cell phone is the main mode of communication, especially among urban residents. Many kiosks offer cell phone use for about 2 soms per unit. If you'll be in Kyrgyzstan a while, it's probably worth it to buy a phone (try Tsum, or the cell phone market at Osh Bazaar in Bishkek), get a SIM card (Sky Mobile (owner of Bitel and Mobi) and Megacom the most popular providers) and sell or give away the phone when you leave.

Internet access is easily available throughout the towns in Kyrgyzstan and hourly rates are low. Speed and services offered depend on the providers.

Food

There are three main types of food in Kyrgyzstan. Most prevalent is Kyrgyz food, based on a nomadic subsistence diet and emphasizing mutton, bread and milk products with little spices. Also common is Uzbek food, characterized by kebabs, noodles, pilafs and stews. Added to this are the common Russian and Chinese entrees.

Some popular dishes include:

Dumlyama (думляма) – Popular in Osh. Large chunks of meat, potatoes, onion, carrot, peppers, cabbage and tomato in a broth.

Borsook – Called the Kyrgyz national bread, it's made into little squares of slightly sweetened fried dough, similar to Russian *hvorost* or Buryat *bobi*.

13

Shorpo – A traditional Kyrgyz boiled meat and potato soup.

Beshbarmak – A dish that means five fingers in Kyrgyz. It is a very traditional entrée and is commonly served at weddings and other celebrations. Noodles with boiled meat, bouillon and fat.

Samsa – Dough filled with meat, fat and onions and baked in a clay oven. Especially popular in the south. Plural is *samsi*.

Manti – Steamed meat (or sometimes pumpkin), fat and onion-filled dumplings.

Oromo – Similar to *manti* but with the addition of potatoes.

Lagman – An Uzbek concoction of noodles in a broth sauce with meat, tomatoes and peppers.

Kurdak – Meat with potatoes and spices

Kishki – Sausage made from intestines and stuffed with meat.

Koumiss – Fermented mare's milk. Alcoholic and very popular, especially in the countryside.

Jarma – Drink made from fermented wheat or corn with kefir added.

Maksim – Similar to *jarma*, but without the kefir. It is left overnight in a warm place to ferment. This drink is popular in hot weather.

Bozo – An alcoholic drink made from fermented wheat. The preparation is difficult.

Chalap – A drink made from kefir, carbonated water and salt.

Chuchvara – Pelmeni, potatoes, meat and veggies in thick, oily lagman-like sauce.

Milk products are popular and include:
> *Sirniki* – Fried cottage cheese patties
> *Blini* – Crepe-like pancakes, often served with sour cream or filled with meat or *tvorog* (cottage cheese)
> *Suzma* – A thick, sour yogurt, eaten with bread and sliced tomatoes.

Sumalak – A brown sweet made from wheat germ sold in small plastic cups. Only women can make it and the many steps include soaking the wheat for three days until it sprouts, grinding it, mixing it with oil, sugar and flour, and cooking it for 24 hours.

Plov – An Uzbek dish of rice cooked in lamb fat with meat, carrots and onions.

Shashlik - Grilled, marinated meat and fat kebabs. Usually served with vinegar, raw onion and *lepeshki*.

Ashlan-foo – Cold noodle dish made with jelly, vinegar and eggs.

Pirozhki – Fried rolls filled with cabbage, potatoes or meat.

Chak-chak – A sweet made from fried dough with honey.

Lepeshka – The most common bread, a round, flat, yeasty bread served warm from a clay oven.

Eid tokoch –A holy bread made in batches of seven. A family will read the Koran, then either eat the bread or give it to neighbors. It is also made after illnesses.

Traditions

Some of the many Kyrgyz traditions include:

- Drinking a cup of tea before eating.
- Making extra food to send guests home with something. At the end of a meal, the host will often provide the guests with plastic bags, then encourage them to clear everything off the table – including vodka, candy, meat, salads, bread and soda.
- After a meal, people cup their hands together to receive and bring them over their face in a washing motion. This is referred to as *omin*. You may also see it done as a signal meaning excuse me, I'm leaving or done by people as they pass cemeteries.
- Putting the right hand over the heart while bowing slightly means thank you.
- Upon marriage, being assigned a third group of parents (called *okul Ata* and *Apa*) who offer advice and try to help the couple stay together. They should be respected as much as real parents.
- *Koumiss* drunk repeatedly from the same horse is said to be healing.
- A host/hostess will only pour a little bit of tea into a cup at a time. In this way, she must refill it frequently and thus demonstrate her concern and respect for her guest. It also means the guests enjoy hotter tea since it must be constantly refilled.
- Giving a public speech before presenting a gift at a wedding. This can be done in groups (families, coworkers, friends, etc.).

- Never throw bread away in a house. It's considered not only rude, but possibly sinful. If the bread is no longer edible, it can be put out in a place where animals can get it, but not thrown away.
- Bread that comes to lie upside down on the table should be turned upright right away.
- Offering bread to visitors. When offered, you should take at least a small bite. This is called *ooz ti*. If you are declining an invitation to stay, you can make the host feel better by at least taking a bit of bread.
- Bringing a gift (such as a cake, other food or flowers) when invited to someone's home.
- A *toi* is a large family celebration. *Tois* can be held to commemorate various events, such as:
  - o*Beshik toi* is the party held 40 days after a child's birth. The infant is considered to have passed the critical stage by then and it's time for the family to officially welcome it into the world and to celebrate its birth.
  - o*Tushoo toi* is the party held when a child reaches a year old. Guests run in a race to cut a cord between the baby's feet.
  - oA circumcision
  - oAn anniversary
  - oA birthday, especially in old age. Fifty years old is a big event and sometimes involves slaughtering a horse.

  If you are invited to a *toi*, you should either bring a gift for the child or some money in an envelope.
- Horse games remain popular, especially during *tois* in rural areas. In the game of *ulak tartysh*, men on horseback compete for a goat's carcass. One team tries to keep the carcass away from the other. They bring the carcass to a ring set up as a goal to score a point. *Oodarysh* is another popular horse game, a type of wrestling on horseback.
- After the birth of a child, the mother and baby stay with the mother's parents. Afterwards, the father's parents hold a small celebration, called a *jentek*, and then the parents can take the baby home.
- Traditional childrearing, still common in rural areas, straps a baby into a wooden baby cradle that has a hole with a cup to collect urine and a little piece of wood hollowed out like a tube to direct the flow for boys. Sometimes a toy or pacifier

will be hung from the handle. When a baby cries, they will untie the arms to allow movement, but keep the legs strapped down. When the mother feeds the baby she doesn't take the child out, but bends down to the crib. This is considered to help keep the baby's legs straight. Babies remain strapped in until they can walk.

•During a funeral it is common to put up a yurt in the family's yard where people gather. It is common to slaughter a horse for the death of a parent.

•During a meal with honored guests, the honored guest could receive the eyeball of the slaughtered animal, carve the head, or give an ear to a child s/he favors. The most honored female usually receives the fat from the sheep's rump.

Words you may hear

Jailoo – High mountain pasture

Marshrutka – Public bus, usually a small van. They can be flagged down anywhere along their route.

Shyrdak – An ornamented, mosaic-like carpet, made from felt.

National holidays

January 1 – New Year's Day

January 7 – Orthodox Christmas

February 23 – Army Day

March 8 – International Women's Day

March 21 – *Nooruz*, Muslim spring festival

March 24 – National Revolution Day, commemorating the 2005 "Tulip Revolution."

May 1 – Labor Day

May 5 – Constitution Day

May 9 – WWII Victory Day

August 31 – Independence Day

November 7 – Revolution Day

Orozo Ait (Eid or Eid ul-Fitr), last day of Ramadan – according to lunar calendar

Khurban Ait (Eid al-Adha) – according to lunar calendar

Events

If you'll be in Kyrgyzstan for a longer time, try to get yourself on the CBT event-mailing list, or get in touch with people from the expat community to find out about trips, festivals and events that are often held, targeting the international residents. These can offer convenient opportunities to visit places in Kyrgyzstan or to learn about cultural highlights. Some festivals to look out for include the Arts and Crafts Festival in Osh (June), the Aitmatov festival in Talas (June), Saimaluu-Tash festival in Kazarman (July), the Felt Festival in Kochkor (July), Honey Processing Festival in Arsalanbob (August), National Games festival in Sarala-Saz jailoo (August), Walnut Collecting Festival in Kara-Suu (October) and the Cotton Festival in Jalalabat (October).

Publications

Non-fiction books

Kyrgyzstan: central asia's island of democracy? By John Anderson is overdue for an updated edition, covering the period only up to 1997. Despite this, it provides a very useful and readable overview of Kyrgyz history, political and economic development and security issues within a compact 100 pages. Filled with lots of useful facts, it's a good primer for visitors who want to understand the country context.

Kyrgyzstan (Lerner Geography Dept., 1993) This book is intended for middle-school readers, but it's a useful introduction to anyone looking for a short overview to the people, land and industry of Kyrgyzstan. Chapters include The Land and People of Kyrgyzstan, Kyrgyzstan's Story, Making a Living in Kyrgyzstan and What's Next for Kyrgyzstan.

Kyrgyzstan by Claudia Antipina, Temirbek Musakeev and Roland Paivo presents a nice collection of photographs, focusing on Kyrgyz textiles and costumes.

The Tulip Revolution: Kyrgyzstan One Year After by Erica Marat presents, in the form of a timeline, a chronology of the 2005-2006 events in Kyrgyzstan and an analysis of the country one year after President Akayev's ouster. This book offers a useful opportunity to understand recent Kyrgyz history.

Shadow of the Silk Road by Colin Thubron takes readers on a modern day trip through the Silk Road territories.

Over the Edge: A True Story of Kidnap and Escape in the Mountains of Central Asia by Greg Child tells the story of four American rock climbers kidnapped near the border with Afghanistan.

Calming the Ferghana Valley: Development and Dialogue in the Heart of Central Asia by Nancy Lubin is a bit outdated, but still useful as an introduction to some of the social, political and economic issues of the south of Kyrgyzstan.

So Many Enemies, So Little Time: An American Woman in All the Wrong Places by Elinor Burkett is a memoir of an American woman's time teaching at a university in Bishkek.

Better a Hundred Friends than a Hundred Rubles? Social Networks in Transition – The Kyrgyz Republic, a World Bank Working Paper by Kathleen Kuehnast and Nora Dudwick provides insight into local culture and relations.

The Lost Heart of Asia by Colin Thubron recounts a journey to Central Asia in the early 1990s.

The Great Game: The Struggle for Empire in Central Asia by Peter Hopkirk is a highly engaging account of the battle between the great powers for the territory of Central Asia.

Turkestan Solo by Ella Maillart is the travel journal of an adventurous female traveler in the 1930s, who crossed Kyrgyzstan and explored many of the major Central Asian cities.

Guidebooks

Kyrgyz Republic by Rowan Stewart has beautiful pictures and top-notch narrative information about Kyrgyzstan.

Lonely Planet Central Asia has a short section on Kyrgyzstan but includes the necessary basics. This book is most useful for those planning to visit several countries in the region.

Kyrgyzstan (The Bradt Guide) is the newest addition to the guidebook collection.

Community Based Tourism (See travel agencies below) has published a guidebook to CBT services. The guide to Bishkek in the appendix is especially useful. Buy a copy for 170 som at CBT offices or download a draft of the 2006 version at: http://www.cbtkyrgyzstan. kg/images/stories/files/Guidebook 2006.pdf.

Maps available in the West include Kyrgyzstan: A Climber's Map and Guide by Garth Willis and Martin Gamache and Kazakhstan, Kyrgyzstan, Tajikistan, Turkmenistan, Uzbekistan Map by GiziMap.

Fiction books

The Kyrgyz epic, Manas, can be found in English translation at souvenir shops in Bishkek.

Any novels by Kyrgyzstan's most famous author, Chingis Aitmatov, will provide a good sense of the local culture and life. Those available in English translation include: The Day Lasts More than a Hundred

Years, Jamilia, The Place of the Skull, Cranes Fly Early and Short Novels.

This is Not Civilization by Robert Rosenberg is a novel set largely in Kyrgyzstan, written by a former Peace Corps volunteer.

Media

A locally produced DVD, **The Amazing Country of Kyrgyzstan** (in English, Russian, French, German and Kyrgyz) provides an overview to Kyrgyzstan. The English recording sounds like a robot reading a Pollyannish Soviet-style text. But the images are beautiful and for someone who has no idea what Kyrgyzstan looks like, this is a good introduction to the most positive aspects of the country. It's available for 700 rubles (no discounts given) on the 4th floor of Tsum or at Beta stores, or contact the producer Vitaliy Podstrechny at cdkyrgyzstan@mail.ru, Tel: 0 (996) 502 56 72 75.

Some of the Kyrgyz music available overseas includes The Music of Kyrgyzstan by Kambarkan Folk Ensemble, Music of Central Asia Vol. 1: Tengir-too Mountain Music of Kyrgyzstan by Tengir-Too and The Silk Road: A Musical Caravan by Various Artists.

The main local papers are *Vecherni Bishkek*, *Komsomolskaya Pravda*, *Dela*, and *Bisnes I Bishkek*.

Films:

Beshkempir: The Adopted Son tells the story of a young boy growing up in the typical local manner, until his best friend, in a burst of anger, reveals that Beshkempir is adopted. The film progresses with little dialogue, moving viewers through the days and weeks of typical village life. Most of the movie is in black and white, with occasional vibrant bursts of color. The relations between individuals, the land and animals are wonderfully conveyed, as is the typical life and cultural practices of Kyrgyz villagers. The movie frankly portrays issues such as early sexual exploration and spousal abuse.

Wedding Chest (Tsunduk Predkov) is about a couple, a French woman and a Kyrgyz man coming back from Paris to Krygyzstan in order to announce their marriage. Some of the scenes are overdone but the scenery is excellent, some cultural traditions and beliefs are illuminated and the reaction of the parents to the foreign bride is indicative of Kyrgyz desire for children to marry within their ethnicity.

Birds of Paradise (Zumak kystary): This Kyrgyz-Kazhak film by Kyrgyz filmmaker Talgat Asyrankulov is about a young, female journalism student who goes to the border to document the issues there and falls in with a comic gang of smugglers. The film feels roughly strung together and the acting is sometimes weak. But the highlight is the famous ostrich farm, located just outside Bishkek, featured in the film.

The PBS documentary on bride stealing by Petr Lom shows three bride kidnappings as they happen. It is a moving and important documentation of this ancient practice that still claims many victims. Watch it online at: http://www.pbs.org/frontlineworld/stories/kyrgyzstan/thestory.html

The documentary *Passes of Matthew*, by Dalmira Tilepbergenova and the DAL-X studio is about the ancient settlements at the bottom of Issyk-Kul lake. It presents the hypothesis of a shrine with relics of Saint Matthew hidden in the deep water near Tyup.

Other movies filmed in Kyrgyzstan, many of them shorts, include:

Pure Coolness (Boz Salkyn) (2007)
Lullaby (2006)
Down from the Seventh Floor (2005) – About the Tulip Revolution.
Saratan (2005)
Altyn Kyrghol (2001)
The Fly Up (Ergii) (2001)
The Chimp (Maimil) (2001)
Sanzhyra (2001)
The White Pony (1999)
Hassan Hussen (1997)
Bus Stop (Beket) (1995)
Taranci (1995)
Jamila (1994) – Based on the Chingis Aitmatov novel.
Sel'kincek (1993)
Where's Your Home, Snail? (Gde tvoy dom, ulitka?) (1992)

Web sites

www.lg.kg has a complete listing of current plays, movies and other goings on, but only in Russian. You can find a complete listing of cafes in Bishkek at http://cafe.lg.kg/.

Local weather, information about Bishkek and Bishkek maps can be found at: http://www.vircity.kg/english.php.

www.Akipress.com provides up-to-the-minute news. Subscribe for full access and for a news digest sent by email.

Ferghana.ru (http://enews.ferghana.ru/) and Eurasianet (http://www.eurasianet.org/index.shtml) are good sources of Central Asian news and analysis.

Transitions Online (http://www.tol.cz/look/TOL/home.tpl?IdLanguage=1&IdPublication=4&NrIssue=267) prints in-depth articles on Central Asia.

The CIA World Factbook (https://www.cia.gov/library/publications/the-world-factbook/geos/kg.html) provides the basic facts and statistics about Kyrgyzstan.

The Kyrgyz government's site is at: http://www.gov.kg/index.php?name=EZCMS&menu=33&page_id=64 and is good for finding some facts about the country.

Many Peace Corps volunteers keep blogs, providing detailed information on life in different parts of Kyrgyzstan. Kyrgyzstan Kid (http://kyrgyzstankid.blogspot.com/) lists several of these and has a notable blog of his own.

Information on Kyrgyzstan is available in Russian at www.welcome.kg.

For information on Central Asia, look at: www.fantasticasia.net.

CHUI REGION

Bishkek

Population: Around one million; phone code: 312

Bishkek is the capital city and the largest city in Kyrgyzstan. It is also by far the most modern and Westernized city in the country. Twenty kilometers wide by twenty kilometers (12.4 by 12.4 miles) in length, the center is compact and lined with leafy trees. Named one of the ten greenest cities of the Soviet Union, it's very pleasant to walk.

The city was founded as the Russian fortress of Pishpek in 1878. From 1926 to 1991 it was called Frunze, after the Bolshevik military leader Mikhail Frunze. If arriving by plane, you'll note the airport code (FRU) is still based on that name.

Sovietskaya, at 32 kilometers (20 miles) long, is the longest street in the city. Manas (also called Baitik Baitira) cuts the city into north and south.

With numerous activites, a wide selection of lodging and restaurants, and the tantalizingly close Tien-Shan mountains, Bishkek is a wonderful place to visit or live.

Look at http://www.vircity.kg/system/pages/map/php/eng vircity2.0/vircity2004v2.0.html?id=373141079 or http://www.signtop.hotmail.ru/photogallery/bishkek/bishkek map.jpg? for an online map of central Bishkek.

Where to Sleep

Bishkek offers a wide range of lodging options, especially in the mid-price range.

Higher End

Holiday Hotel (ul. Abdrahmanov 204A; Tel: 902900; Fax: 902923; hotel@holiday.kg; www.holiday.kg) is a sparkling new red and blue hotel, the bright colors that were so infrequently seen in Soviet times. Located right across from the Hyatt, it's a good choice for people who want comfort and a central location for about half the price of the Hyatt. The rooms are a bit small, but neat and clean, with a small, flat screen TV, and modern bathrooms. Singles cost 3600 som, double 4200, luks (including bathrobes and a second room) 4800 and a suite 5500. Credit cards accepted.

The fanciest option in town is the **Hyatt Regency** (ul. Sovietskaya 19, near the Opera and Ballet Theater; Tel: 661234; www.bishkek.hyatt.com). But unless you are a devotee of luxury, it's hard to justify parting with $265-$565 (plus 26% tax) for a room without breakfast (which will cost you an extra $25) given the good selection of comfortable, safe hotels in Bishkek.

**The Silk Road Lodge (ul. Abdumoichnova 229; Tel: 661129; Fax: 661655; silroad@infotel.kg; www.silkroad.com.kg) looks like a castle, with grey and mauve turrets rising from the center of town. It's centrally located, within walking distance of parks, shops and restaurants. Rooms cost 84 euro for a single, 92 euro for a double, 100 for a *luks* and 112 euro for a *luks* apartment. Many people who want a nice place for less than the Hyatt stay here.

Another luxury option is the four-star **Ak-Keme** (sometimes called the **Pinara**) (93 Prospekt Mira; Tel: 540143/44/45/52, 541790, 542318, 540277; Fax: 542365; 542408; 542404; 484464; www.akkemehotel.com; Bishkek@akkemehotel.com). It has much more of a Soviet feel than the Hyatt or some of the other newer hotels, but is nicer than the Dostuk. It's located in the outer area of town, not far from the U.S. embassy. Rates are $160 for a single, $220 double, $300 suite and $500 presidential suite, including continental breakfast.

The **Golden Dragon** (ul. Elebaev 60; Tel: 902771; Fax: 902773; GDHotel@saimanet.kg; http://www.gdhotel.kg/main/) is a 42-room hotel located 10 minutes outside of the city. Rooms include internet, satellite TV, safe deposit boxes and mini-bars. There is a spa, restaurant and business center in the hotel. Airport pickup available. $125 single, $150 double, $175 deluxe, $400 suite.

Mid-level

The **MBA International Business Center (237 ulitsa Panfilova (just off of Frunze); Tel: (996 312) 623 120; 623 122; Fax: (996 312) 660 638; center@amp.aknet.kg; www.amp.aknet.kg/hotel) is a classy, comfortable hotel that caters to foreigners. Singles run $60, doubles $76, including a breakfast of your choice delivered to the room. Within walking distance of central areas. The lower floors of the same building offer more run-down, unremodeled rooms for much cheaper.

The **Kyrgyz Altyn** (Prospekt Manas 30 (near intersection with Toktogul); Tel: 66-64-12, 66-61-14) hotel is very centrally located and for Kyrgyz citizens, offers great value. Unfortunately, prices for foreigners are much higher. Singles start at 1150 som, doubles at 1840 and half-*lux* 2300 and *lux* rooms, with a bedroom, living room and bathroom cost 2760 (2300 on the upper floors – there is no lift). Rooms are clean and comfortable, but don't come with breakfast, nor have the nice touches that should come with that price. For instance, you have to put the sheets and blankets on the bed yourself and the toilet paper is the brown cardboard kind. Nevertheless, if a central location is a priority, the Kyrgyz Altyn is a decent choice. There is a café on the first floor.

Shumkar Asia Guest House (ul. Osipenko 34; Tel: 272105; shumkar-asia@inbox.ru) has 11 rooms with private bath, fridge and TV. Rates are 1722 som/single, 2460 som/double and 2952/suite, including breakfast.

**Asia Mountains Guesthouse (ul. Lineinaya 1-a; Tel: 996 (312) 690234, 690235; 69-40-75; Fax: 996 (312) 69-02-36; aljona@mail. elcat.kg, asiamountains@mail.ru; http://www.asiamountains.co.uk/ english.html, www.asiamountains.elcat.kg) is an attractive 12-room chalet with a swimming pool and views of snow-capped mountains. The rooms are cozy, with furniture made from natural wood, cable TV, A/C, refrigerator and modern bathrooms with hot water. The facilities feel secure. The main disadvantage is location, positioned at the end of a dark, potholed street, with no restaurants nearby. Meals can be ordered at the hotel, but only in advance and when the hotel doesn't have events scheduled. Prices ($30 for a single, $40 for double and $50 for an apartment, discounts for longer stays) include a cold but substantial breakfast.

Another centrally located budget option, with singles at $36, doubles $48 (including breakfast), is **Hotel Alpiniste (ul. Panfilov 113 (between Kulatova and Gorki); Tel/Fax: 996-312-595647, 699621; alpinist@elcat.kg; http://www.alpinisthotel.centralasia.kg/). They have 19 rooms, as well as a 50-place conference hall, dry cleaning services, and private security services. Internet available for 60 som/hour or from room.

The **Hotel Dostuk** (ulitsa Frunze 429, at intersection with Pravda; Tel: 284251), the premier hotel in Soviet times, has seen better days, but still stands as one of Bishkek's high-rise lodgings. Rooms cost 3150 som for a single, 3780 for a double, including breakfast. Credit cards accepted.

The mid-range **Hotel Ordu** (ulitsa Kudruka 107, near Maladaya Gvardiya; Tel: 218922) has rooms from $50-100.

Hotel Semetei (ulitsa Toktogul 125, at intersection with Logvinenko; Tel: 218324) looks like a military hotel, but is open to all and offers a good value option in the center of town. Rooms are 1200 som.

"Guest House" (ul. Koenkozova 6, between Moscovskaya and Bokonbaevo); Tel: 699900; Fax: 690914) is centrally located. Rooms cost $50 for a single, $70 for a double.

Budget

Salima (237 ulitsa Panfilova, in same building as MBA International Business Center above; Tel: 623107) is one of the best-value choices, with simple but safe rooms from $10/night.

For a cheap sleep, try the **Hotel Kazakhstan** (Tel: 65-47-59 or 65-98-10), located next to the *avtovokzal*, bus station. It's also one of the closet options to the airport. Built in January 2005, you can get a clean bed in a four-person room (there may not be anyone else in there) with a TV, fridge and bathroom with hot water for 300 som. Beds cost 300-600 som, rooms 1200-2000. The hotel doesn't have a separate price list for foreigners and seems to appreciate business, even in the middle of the night. From the airport, take *marshrutka* 153 or 350 to the intersection with Vasilivsky trakt, then walk 4-6 blocks or take marshrutka 114 to the hotel.

Sary-Chelek (Orozbekova and Frunze; Tel: 215877) has rooms for 600-700 som/person/night.

Sabyrbek's B&B (ul. Razzakova 21, near Moscovskaya, across from German embassy; Tel: 621398; http://www.sabyrbek.com/) is a budget deal at $5-10 per person to stay in a centrally located private home.

Ultimate Adventure (see travel agencies below) runs a guesthouse (185 ul. Kurienkeva, at intersection with Serova; near Jibek Jolu and Togolok Moldo; Tel: 270754; mobile: 0502 222634; ultiadv.mail.kg) with singles for 17 euros and doubles and triples for 14 euro/person, including breakfast.

Bed and Breakfasts are offered by **CBT Kyrgyzstan** (see Other Services below; http://www.cbtkyrgyzstan.kg/index.php?option=com_content&task=view&id=21&Itemid=38) for 1000-1500 som per night and **Kyrgyz Concept** (see Other Services below; http://eng.concept.kg/hotels/bed_and_breakfast/) for $25-35/day.

If you'll be staying in Bishkek for a longer period, **renting an apartment** is the best value.

- A private landlord offers 2-3 room apartments for $10-$20/night (Baitik Batira 39, near Sovietskaya; Tel: 544474, 0502612914; Fax: 544964).
- **Kyrgyz Concept** (http://eng.concept.kg/hotels/flats/) offers a variety of rentals.
- **Absolut** rental agency (http://www.absolut.org.kg/?lang=eng) is known for Western-standard apartments.

•Some landlords ask for payment several months in advance. If this is the case, see if you can negotiate a reduced price for advance payment.

For those living in Bishkek, it's easy to find domestic services, whether housekeeping or childcare. Often, landlords will recommend people. Tanya (Tel: 604203) and Natasha (Tel: 978184) proved trustworthy and reliable. Ask around for recommendations.

Where to Eat

Bishkek has a vast selection of cafes and restaurants, with new choices opening frequently.

Pizza

Dolce Vita Pizzeria (ul. Ahunbaeva 116a; Tel: 54-39-84; Open 11-12) has some of the best thin-crust pizza in Kyrgyzstan (60-250 som). Good selection of vegetables and salads. Nice patio and friendly, fast service. Delivery costs 70 som and takes about 40 minutes. Accessible by taking marshrutka 160 to Ahunbaeva, then continuing walking in the direction the bus goes. The café is on the right.

Doka Café (ul. Ahunbaeva 97a, near ul. Baitik Batira; and ul. Kievskaya 153, near Manas; Tel: 695555; www.doka.kg) is a popular place for pizza.

New York Pizza (ul. Kievskaya 89; Tel: 662644, 664871, 909909) has mediocre pizza. Delivery available 24 hours.

Italian

The Italian restaurant, **Adriatico (219 Chui Avenue (between Togolok Moldo and Isanov streets); Tel: 217632) is one of the best in town, featuring a real Italian chef. The veal with mushrooms, fresh fish, and grilled tomatoes and eggplant are all sensational. The service is very attentive and each meal ends with a free tasty mini milkshake. A good place to take a special guest. Expect to spend 400-500 som per person.

Cyclone is a medium-priced Italian restaurant in the center of town (136 Prospekt Chui, near intersection with Togolok Moldo; Tel: 21-28-66;). It is popular among foreigners.

East European/Russian

****Korchma** (ul. Riskulova 12; Tel: 21-19-53; from the intersection of Chui and Manas, walk north along Manas, take the first right (onto Riskulova), it's on the right side) is a cozy, modest café serving national

Ukrainian food. The seven tables are set in a comforting atmosphere with carved wood decorations and clay dishware. The heavy menu, in Russian and English, offers such delights as homemade berry juice, *vareniki* with a variety of fillings, and many options for both vegetarians and meat eaters. A nice place for a date or a gathering with a small group of friends. A meal costs 300-400 per person.

Walk through the clay wine pitcher at the entrance of **Mimino (ul. Kievskaya 27, near intersection with Pravda; Tel: 661375) to find a wonderful selection of authentic Georgian cuisine. Excellent vegetarian options include eggplant with beans and pomegranate seeds, cheese-filled bread, and mushrooms. Expect to spend about $10 per person plus 10% gratuity and 40 som/person for live, often blaring, music.

Restoran Moldova (ul. Turusbekova 49; Tel: 213568; Open 9-22) and the underground, pleasantly cavelike **Restoran Primevara** (ul. Toktogula 175, near Manas; Tel: 211726; Open 9-22) are popular places for Moldovan food. In the early 2000s, they were among the nicest restaurants in Bishkek. Entrees 150-200 som, open daily.

Asian

Santa Maria is an upscale, recently remodeled restaurant on Chui and Togolok Moldo (Tel: 610532, 212484), serving high-quality Italian, Korean and Japanese food. English menu. The pumpkin soup is great, as is the marinated Korean beef *pulkogi*. A picture menu helps make ordering the Korean easier. Expect to spend 400 som and up.

Tsi San (ulitsa Sovietskaya, across from ZAGS and near the circus) is a Chinese restaurant with large portions that attract the local Chinese. The salads are good, entrees heavy on the oil and vinegar. A meal runs 125 som.

Putushestvie Sinbada (ul. Pravda between Chui and Frunze, open daily from 10) is a decent Chinese restaurant.

Jihua Chinese Muslim Cafeteria (ulitsa Pravda, near intersection with Frunze, right next to Café Beirut; Tel: 0502-820888; 0312-29-36-62) is a neat, clean, and friendly café with a solid base of Chinese patrons. Food is tasty, though typically oily. Good selections for vegetarians. About 250 som/person

Some of the best Chinese food in Bishkek can be found at **Shao Lin (ul. Zhibek Zholy 372, near intersection with Isanova; Tel: 21-47-37; mobile: 0502-307899). Fresh, delicious food, good service, and reasonable prices. You can eat well for 200 som. A nice place to visit with a group.

Pekinskaya Utka cafe (Chui Prospekt 138, near Togolok Moldo, across from Adriatico; Tel: 21-36-76 or 0502 57 82 63; Open

10:30-23) is a Chinese restaurant popular with locals. Salads cost 40-100 som, soups 20-30, fish 100-400, chicken 90-200 and beef and mutton 90-250. There are several vegetarian options available and a menu in English and Russian. Pekinskaya Utka also has a more formal restaurant on ul. Baitik Batira 29 (on ul. Sovietskaya, between Communisticheskaya and Druzhba; Tel: 54-29-82, 0555 507982).

Tet-A-Tet (ul. Ibraimova 146a; Tel: 62-39-73) serves up traditional Korean food, cooked right in front of you. Good vegetarian options. Expect to spend a steep 500-800 som.

Pick up Chinese in a hurry at **Chinatown**, on Erkindik and Jibek Jolu.

Aoyama Sushi bar (93 Toktogula and Erkindek; Tel: 623053) is one of the most expensive restaurants in Bishkek.

American

The **Cowboy Café** (ul. Orozbekov 62, between Kievskaya and Toktogula; Tel: 661823; disco from 8 p.m. daily) serves up surprisingly authentic western burgers, American steaks, milkshakes and salads by servers in black vests and cowboy hats. In the evening, see the waiters dance. Prices are similar to what you'd pay in the U.S. Good for those missing a taste of home.

**The Metro Bar and Grill (Prospect Chui 168a, between Turusbekova and Manas; Tel: 217664) is one of the most popular expat hangouts, with frequent events and a good selection of burgers, pizza, salads, chicken fingers and mains. It also has the best selection of new books in English for sale in Bishkek.

European

Crostini at The Hyatt (ulitsa Sovietskaya 19, near the Opera and Ballet Theater; Tel: 661234; http://bishkek.regency.hyatt.com/hyatt/hotels/entertainment/restaurants/index.jsp) is the place to go when you are tired of national food and want a taste of Europe. You can find great soups here (including gazpacho), club sandwiches, calamari, and elegant desserts. The high tea, served Wednesdays and Saturdays from 3 to 6 is a good deal – 450 som for all you can eat canapés, desserts and tea. Sunday brunch is served from 11-3 for 1250 som (children 50% off). Credit cards accepted.

FatBoys (104 Chui Prospekt) is bright and colorful, with the feeling of a foreigner's watering hole. The dominant language among patrons is English. The breakfast menu is especially impressive and several rare treats on the menu include burritos, hummus, baked potatoes, pizza and Greek yogurt. Prices are reasonable with a meal running 100-150 som. But the food is mediocre at best and the service sullen, making it less attractive than many other options.

Chili Steak House (Alma-Atinskaya 169/Zhibek Zholy; Tel: 433149, 290332) is an upscale, expensive establishment that focuses on high quality, and often spiced, meat. Expect to spend 300-500 som.

Captain Nemo (ul. Togolok Moldo 14, near Toktogul; Tel: 627812; captain_nemo@list.ru;) has the reputation for the best coffee in Bishkek and very good fish. For those staying the area, Captain Nemo will order coffee from overseas for you. Good vegetarian selections, as well as fish, pork, beef and chicken. Menu in English and Russian. Credit cards accepted. Entrees average 150 som.

Café Boulevard (41/10 Erkindik boulevard (on corner of Kievskaya; Tel: 661698; café.boulevard@gmail.com) is a new café geared to expatriate visitors. It is the first café to offer wireless Internet connections, where you can come and drink a cup of coffee while working or reading. It also offers a full menu, including Baskin-Robbins ice cream and ice tea. The food is good, especially the Caeser salad and the French cakes, though service is slow.

Coffee (ul. Manas and Moskovskaya) is a new coffee shop.

**Café Okean (pr. Manasa 61; Tel: 610888) is a wonderful, upscale seafood restaurant with fun, bright decorations and good quality eats.

**Bar Navigator (ulitsa Moscovskaya, near intersection with Razakova; Tel: 665151, 66-45-45; cnavigator@yandex.ru; http://www.navigator-cafe.kg) is a higher-end restaurant, popular with foreigners. The menu is in English and Russian and offers an especially wide choice of healthy salads. The fish is very good. Entrees average about 260 som; home delivery available for 100 som.

As long as you are not in a hurry, **Triada (ul. Toktugula 230, near intersection with Kalyk Akieva; Tel: 655204) is a wonderful restaurant for quality food at reasonable prices. You can have a good lunch for under $3 by ordering a salad and a side dish. Veggie lovers will appreciate the delicious cauliflower and the mushroom soup.

Steinbrau (ul. Gertzena 5) is run by a family of ethnic Germans and is a popular place to drink freshly brewed beer, together with German and European food.

Mixed

****Stari Edgar** (west side of Russian Drama theater; tel: 664408) is a cozy, underground café with an impressive selection of entrees and salads, including rabbit pizza and the unusually healthy for Bishkek chicken breasts with spinach. Live music nightly from 7, except Sunday, when there is a pianist. Outdoor seating available in summer.

Café Shoola (ul. Sovietskaya, between ul. Toktogul and Moscovskaya) is a relatively new café and especially popular at night. The comfortable and casual atmosphere attracts locals and foreigners. It features a large and varied menu in Russian and in English, good service, and reasonable prices (most items 40-100 som).

Café Vis a Vis (ul. Logvinenko and Chui; Tel: 666846) is a busy and comfortable place, with wooden tables and entrees from 80-100 som. Open daily.

U Mazaya (ul. Sovietskaya 199; near Zhibek Zholu; Tel: 665-081) and **U Bolshovo Mazaya (ul. Toitonbaeva 29; near Zhukeeva-Pudovkina; Tel: 959-272; take the 170 marshrutka uphill from Mos/Soviet) are famous for two things – rabbit and a menu of almost 200 cocktails. Their *shashlik* is also wonderful. Warm, welcoming atmosphere, excellent service, live music, dancing, lots of choice (including vegetables, like cauliflower fried in egg) and beautiful layered cocktails that look like striped sand. On Fridays, Saturdays and Sundays from 6-8, cocktails are 50% off and the bartender puts on a fantastic performance, later auctioning off the drink he makes. Will deliver.

Sweet 60s (Bulvar Molodoi Gvardii 44, near ul. Kievskaya; Tel: 653322) is a new café, with live music nightly from 8. It's a calm version of a 50s café, better to visit for the drinks and the music than the American, Italian and Mexican food. About 100 som. 20% discount between 11 and 3.

Café Express (next to Bereket on ul. Moscovskaya and Krasni Oktybrskaya) offers Chinese, European and national food at excellent value. Most entrees under 70 som. Unpretentious and packed with locals throughout the day.

**The Four Seasons Restaurant (116a Tynystanov Street, across from Russian Drama Theater; Tel: 621548) is classy, comfortable and upscale, with good-quality entrees averaging 200-300 som. The menu offers a lot of choice, including Chinese food (the beef with black mushrooms is fantastic), *shashlik*, meats, salads and ice cream. Pizzas, ranging in price from 150-240 som, are available for delivery for an 80 som fee. The menu is in Russian and English with colorful pictures. In the summer, comfortable chairs and tables are arranged around a fountain. Credit cards accepted.

Café Saamalik (Саамалык) (ulitsa Pravda, near the intersection with Moscovskaya) is a 24-hour, moderately priced café, serving local dishes, including salads (15-45 som), soups (15-30 som), Asian food (20-40 som), meats (45-65 som), fish (45-55 som) blini and ice cream. It's not a low fat place. Most items are slathered in mayo and sour cream.

Café Riviera (ulitsa Gogol, near intersection with Chui Prospekt) is popular with locals. The service is fast and attentive, the food tasty and good value. Try to arrive before 8 when blaring live music makes conversation virtually impossible. Salads 40-60 som, most entrees 60-120. Open from 12 to 3. A restaurant by the same name is located upstairs.

Irahat (Ырахат) (ul. Ivraimova 105, across from the Dostuk hotel; Open 8-24 daily) has a huge selection, including national foods, milk products, European and Chinese, served by tuxedoed waiters on red velvet tablecloths. It's a good place for a meal and an especially nice place for a gathering. Tables for groups are beautifully set in the atmosphere of faded elegance. Salads 40-60, most entrees 60-90, music 20 som/person after 6 p.m., service 5% day/10% night.

La Carte (ul. Toktogula 95, at intersection with Erkendik); Tel: 0555-59-95-95; 0555-94-20-50; lacarte@elcat.kg;), opened in 2007, is the newest addition to the luxury café market. With a logo of "Thanks God that Im VIP," it's more of a place to go just because one can. And for that reason, it can be an interesting place to look at those who can afford to spend $15 on lunch (or $30-50 for dinner) in Bishkek. The décor, representing three different styles, is opulent. But the food is just mediocre, especially for the price.

Café Arbat (ul. Unusalieva (formerly Karl Marx) 91; Tel: 512094, 512087) is a great place for a group. The upstairs restaurant is located in newly remodeled room, stylishly decorated in pale blue and ivory. The large menu offers a wide selection of European and national food. There is a dance hall at one end of the café, as well the **1980s discotheque** downstairs.

Café Aidai (Айдай) (across from KarVen club on the intersection of ulitsas Gogol and Toktogula) has a large selection (ask for the pictures) and good quality food, though sometimes greasy. The fish and tomato kebabs are especially good. Salads range from 40-50 som, most entrees are 40-90. There is a 15 som charge for music between 6 and 11 p.m. and a 7% service charge.

TimeOut (ul. .Togolok Moldo and ul. Ryskulove, next to Spartak Stadium) is an upscale restaurant, serving local and international food, and popular for evening drinks.

The **Monarch** (ul. Ahunbaeva 46a, near intersection with Ordzhinkde), located in the site of a former nightclub, is a recommended restaurant.

Apelsin (ul. Togolok Moldo 17/1; Tel: 622477, 622483) is a modern, upscale restaurant with a variety of foods and good facilities for children during the day. At night, it's a popular place for adults to gather.

Kyrgyz/Uzbek

**Jalalabat (on the corner of ulitsa Kievskaya and Togolok Moldo) is a must experience – an ornate, traditional Southern eatery, filled with the scent of smoking kebabs and warm *lepushka*. Moderate prices. In summer, sit on a tapchan outside and enjoy the people watching.

**Panorama (12th microrayon) offers a great view of the city over dinner.

Faiza (ul. Zhibek Zholu 555; near Manas; Tel: 663747); known as the best Kyrgyz food, packed at lunchtime, take-out available. Worth a visit for the character.

Café Admiral (ul. Toktogul and Manas) has juicy, spicy *shashlik*. Menu in Russian and English, good service, comfortable outdoor seating in summer, but can be a long wait. Expect to spend 200-400 som. Live music at night.

Café Arzu (ul. Zhibek Zholy, on the outskirts of Bishkek (*storoni Tokmok*), past the Alamedinski market) is an Uighur café with a great atmosphere, especially in summer. It's not worth coming for the mediocre food (at least it's cheap – nothing on the menu is over 100 som). Instead, come for the good live music, dancing, and fun. Popular with young adults and parties. Get there by taxi from the city center (80-100 som) or take marshrutka 344 on ul. Chui from Tsum or 1000 Melochi. The owner has a café by the same name in New York City (http://nymag.com/listings/restaurant/cafe-arzu/).

Café Concord (74 ul. Orozbekova; right on the central square; Tel: 661817) is designed to resemble the interior of an airplane, with staff dressed in flight attendant clothing and caps. Pretend to take off, while looking out at the activities of the central square. Come for the decor, not the greasy food. The business lunch, served from 11-3, costs less than 100 som. Prices at other times are a bit higher. Flight regime: Take-off at 10 a.m., landing at 12 a.m.

Café Rohat (Chui Prospekt and Alamedinski; walk down Alamadinski past Caravan Sarai Café, Rohat is 200 meters further down) is a clean, pleasant café, good for group events.

Stariy Gorod (ul. Lev Tolstoi at intersection with ul. Chapaeva; not far from Molodaya Gvardiya) is designed in an Uzbek-Kyrgyz style. The food is good and the restaurant hosts oriental shows every evening.

There are several nice but inexpensive cafes on ulitsa Gogola, near Chui Prospekt, serving up local food for 20-50 som. Both indoor and outdoor seating available.

Bishkek Time (Бишкек Тайм), located next to the post office on Chui Prospekt (Open from 8 to 11 Monday-Saturday), is worth a visit for the unique Soviet art on carved wall panels depicting traditional Kyrgyz games. From the left, the first panel shows *alaman baiga*, a horse race competition between regions. The third pictures *kiskumai*, a game in which a man and woman race. Before crossing the finish lane, the man must kiss the woman. If he fails, the woman can chase him with a whip on the return trip. *Erkise* is shown on the fourth panel, a tradition of passing a drink within a group, especially at weddings. Whoever gets the cup must take a drink, then tell a story. The sixth panel shows *berkuche*, a man training a falcon to hunt.

Turkish

**Yusa (ul. Lagvinenko 14, near intersection with Bokonbaevo; Tel: 62 38 37) is a warm, busy restaurant, where friendly staff run back and forth serving up fresh, hot Turkish food, including kebabs, pizzas, salads and soups. Menu in Turkish, Russian and English, without much description, though the salads and some grilled meats are available for viewing. Around 200-300 som.

Next door to the Kyrgyz Turkish Manas University, **Café Sem Sem (7 7)** (on Manas, near intersection with Akmatbek Jumanbaev, on left when going uphill) is a nice, comfortable café where you can eat authentic Turkish food – dolma, kebab, sweets and salads, for under 100 som. Open 8-11.

Middle Eastern

**Café Beirut (ulitsa Pravda 105, near intersection with Frunze; across from Hotel Dostuk; Tel: 29-36-71) is one of the great finds in Bishkek, serving fantastic curried *sudak*, falafel, smooth, garlicy hummus and other Lebanese delicacies. Sometimes the service is slow, but the food is worth the wait. The maza, or appetizer selection, can make a good meal – 350 som for 2 or 3, 650 for 4. Entrees 120-220 som. Menu in English and Russian. Take-out available.

**Ozhak Kebab Café (Dzerzhinskaya 27; Tel: 0502-747871) is an unassuming place, located across from a green park. This cafe offers only kebab. But for 100-150 som per person, you can eat a full meal, including kebab, salad and accompaniments

Indian

Bombay Restaurant (Chui Prospekt 110; Tel: 625115) is an upscale Indian restaurant, with matching décor. Good service and food, for about $10 per person. Open daily.

Self service

There are lots of little cafes and fast food kiosks around the fountains outside TSUM.

Narodni supermarkets dot the city. **Beta Stores** (ulitsa Chui 150A; the corner of Chui and Isanov) is the famous and extensive Turkish supermarket that was looted during the March 2005 revolution. The newly reconstructed and opened shop has become a tourist attraction. A fountain and series of benches outside the store make it a nice place for a picnic lunch or snack. **Ramstore** (ulitsa Gorkovo 27/1) is the newest addition to the scene, located in the fancy **Vefa shopping center**. It has a nice selection of prepared salads and foods.

Ak Emir (corner of ulitsa Moskovskaya and Shopokov, not far from Soviet) is the most central and most expensive bazaar. But it features a beautiful selection of fruits, vegetables, nuts, meats, sweets and prepared salads for do-it-yourself catering.

You can pick up a quick snack at **Mir Blini**, at the busstand near Sovietskaya and Kievskaya. 8-16 som.

Zhivie Soki is a great, fresh fruit and vegetable juice, made daily. It can be found at Beta-Stores, some Narodni stores, Aristocrat or by order. Tel: 273921, 411117, 785907; vittoll@mail.ru.

Warm, flaky *samsi* are available on the corner of Togolok Moldo and Chui for about 10 som.

The People of Kyrgyzstan – Bishkek Shopkeeper

One morning my friend Zhenya invited me over for home-baked pizza. Her 9:30 a.m. call pulled me out of bed on a Saturday.

"Come on over!" she said. "I'm already starting to cook."

When I arrived shortly after 11, her apartment smelled of dough. The pizza was almost done. She'd topped the thick, pastry-like dough with mushrooms, tomatoes, cheese, pineapple, black olives and ham.

Over thick, gooey slices of pizza, she told me about her new store, selling cosmetics, toys, dishes and personal care products, in operation for four months. She had hired two salesgirls, sisters.

She complained that one was illiterate and she wanted to replace her. She pulled out the accounts to show me. She'd corrected all the salesgirl's mistakes with green pen – changing *malako* to the correct *moloko* (milk), changing spasm to jigsaw puzzle. She made all kinds of mistakes that even I, as a non-native Russian speaker, could probably avoid.

"If she was Kyrgyz, I could understand," Zhenya said. "But she's Russian. I asked her if she went to school and she said yes, but I can't believe it. She's illiterate."

Zhenya controlled the store. She opened and closed it and traveled almost daily to the Dordoi market to fetch products needed to resupply the shelves.

"I need to go there after lunch to stock up on things for the March 8th holiday," she said. She expected high demand for cosmetics and perfume before International Women's Day and invited me to accompany her to the market. Since I needed clothes for my belly dancing class, I readily agreed to accompany her.

We set off for the market in gorgeous, sunny, spring-like weather. People seemed to walk with a lighter step, as if the newly green branches of the willow extended its new life to the city residents. We boarded a *marshrutka* and stayed on until the last stop. Dordoi, a huge mass of giant, double-stacked iron shipping containers (the lower one used as a store and the upper one for storage), is located on the edge of the city. Stretching over more than a kilometer, it is one of the great markets of Asia and a major entry point of Chinese goods to Central Asia and Russia.

Many people make their living at Dordoi, from struggling small entrepreneurs to incredibly wealthy traders. A metal container can sell for as much as $40,000. The boxes, freezing cold in winter and burning hot in summer, provide many with a path to security and/or wealth.

On the last weekend before March 8th, considered one of the biggest holidays of the year, buyers packed the market. We walked into the mayhem. We heard men yelling *kosh* (the same word used to move cows out of the way) as they pushed wheelbarrows of goods through the crowd and felt the wheels nab at our ankles. We heard a chorus of simultaneous bargaining, bags opened and filled, pockets opening to remove or accept wrinkled Kyrgyz, Kazakh and U.S. bills.

"My God, look at the dishes row," Zhenya said. People thronged the rows like ants around a fresh crumb. When Zhenya stopped momentarily, the crowd jostled us: a baby cart filled with round loaves of *lepushka*, a young boy pushing a cart he'd fill with goods, a man selling meat-filled *samsi* out of plastic bags. There was no room for stopping.

I found what I needed, then we went to purchase items for Zhenya's store. It was my first time shopping with a vendor. I knew thousands of people did the same thing as Zhenya every day – came to Dordoi to find items they could sell at a higher margin in the city center. I enjoyed seeing how she went about it.

"Let's get out of here," she said, referring to the Turkish section of the market. "It's too expensive. The cheapest place is where the Chinese vendors sell their things. Not many people know about it yet."

We went to another part of the market, where indeed, almost all the vendors were Chinese. They spoke broken, barely comprehensible Russian. But they were friendly, helpful, and sold cheap goods for rock-bottom prices.

"How much are these wholesale?" Zhenya asked, pointing at some nylons.

"Ten som," a short Chinese man said. That was 25 cents.

"I'll take 120," Zhenya said.

She leaned over to me. "I can sell them for 40 som," she said.

Behind the counter, I saw some plastic bags with the Dollar Store logo. The market was like a giant dollar store, but with most of the goods under a quarter instead of a dollar.

Next she bought 30 bottles of nail polish for 30 cents each, followed by imitation Nivea and L'oreal mascara, glittering Chinese eyeshadow, flowered hair ties for 20 cents each, bracelets for mere pennies, ribbons and perfume.

The Chinese imitation perfumes and cosmetics used very convincing packaging. Only the grammatical mistakes in the English text identified them as knockoffs, but the locals would never notice.

Zhenya told me about a Kyrgyz man who recently came in to buy perfume for the holiday.

"He was looking at the different bottles and trying to decide which to buy. He asked me where it was from. I told him Poland."

"You lied?" I asked. I frequently asked where the goods I bought were from and hoped I received honest answers.

"I can't say China. If I say China, nobody will buy my goods. Everyone is afraid to buy Chinese goods. They are afraid of poor quality. However, it should be obvious to him that it's a Chinese product. If it was original perfume, Chanel or Christian Dior, it wouldn't cost $1.25 and it wouldn't be packaged in a plastic container inside the box."

I frowned. How would a Kyrgyz who has never seen an original Chanel know?

"So he bought all five perfumes," she continued, "saying he'd let his women choose which one they liked best. He bought one for his mother, wife, daughters. It was good for both of us. He thought he got a Polish product and I sold my goods with a 100% markup."

She smiled. The first few months involved some trial and error as she figured out what people wanted and how much they'd pay. But with time she was gaining confidence and seemed to be having fun.

What to Do

Museums

The **Fine Arts Museum (196 Sovietskaya; Tuesday-Sunday 9-5) is located in a decaying concrete hulk of a building, but it is well worth a visit, exhibiting a nice array of local Kyrgyz artists and woven goods from a full collection of over 17,000 works. Some paintings are available for sale on the left of the first floor, as is a selection of tourist-oriented books, some in English and German. Admission is 100 for foreign adults, 20 for foreign students and 20 for local adults. Open Tuesday-Sunday 10-6, Friday 11-5.

The **Historical Museum (Ala-Too Square) (open 10-1 and 2-7; entrance: 45 som) is worth a visit, especially for the fantastic cultural murals painted across the ceilings. The first floor has a display of national clothes, the second is the obligatory Soviet revolutionary section, lightened with impressive bronze statue scenes, and the third floor displays Kyrgyz archeology, texts, jewelry and folklore. There is a giftshop near the entrance.

An outdoor **gallery** displays **local art** for sale near Ala-Too square. Some are just vendors, others are the actual artists. Many artists, including Boris (0502 126645), are willing to take orders. Nearby is the **Open Air Sculpture Museum** (346 Frunze), set up in 1984 for the Kyrgyz Republic's 60th anniversary. Sculptors across the former Soviet Union sent pieces for the theme of peace and labor.

The **Frunze Museum** (Ul. Frunze) includes the home where Mikhail Frunze, the Bolshevik military leader that Bishkek was named after during Soviet times was born and raised. The museum provides a useful survey of Bishkek and the Kyrgyz republic during the Soviet Republic, including the role of Frunze.

Theater

The **Tunguch Theater** (also referred to as the former Americanski Pop) (intersection of Chui and Turkobekova; Tel: 217527) puts on some interesting local performances, including the first Kyrgyz musical. Stop by to check the schedule. The attached restaurant, Metro Pub, is a nice place for a meal or a drink after the show.

Regular performances of varying quality take place at the **Opera and Ballet Theater** house (ul. Abdyrahmanova 167, next to Hyatt; Tel: 640088, 661841, 661548).

Cinema

The best movie theaters in Bishkek, and in Kyrgyzstan, are the **Octybr** theater (Pr. Chui 184; Tel: 655629, 655612; kino.in.kg) and Vefa (Vefa Shoping Center, ul. Gorkovo 21/1, Tel: 596688). Both have comfortable seats and large screens. Tickets cost 100-150 som.

The **Puppet Theater** (Sovietskaya and Mmichurina) offers performances on Sundays at 11 a.m.

The **Russian drama theater (ul. Tynystanova 122; Tel: 662032, 621571) presents regular, often very good performances. The **Kyrgyz drama theater** (273 Panfilov, behind the Government House, Tel: 665717, 665802, 216958) presents shows in the local languages.

Music

The **Kyrgyz State Philharmonic (253 Chui, near Manas; Tel: 212235, 212262) has two concert halls offering a variety of performances, from classic to pop. Call or check akipress.org for schedules.

The **Conservatory** (ul. Jantosheva 115; Tel: 479542) presents concerts by professors and students.

Contact the **Cultural Fund Sahna (ul. Ibraimova 24; Tel: 428112, 426508; Fund_sakhna@yahoo.com) to see if the experimental theater group, led by Nurlan Asanbekov, has any upcoming shows. If so, it is well worth seeing, a wonderful collage of art and music, enjoyable even without any understanding of Kyrgyz.

Volunteer

A reputable and worthy charity, based in Bishkek (but serving both Bishkek and Batken), is **Babuskha Adoption (ul. Moscovskaya 39-5 (near Pravda); Tel/Fax: 680118; babushka@elcat.kg; dina@babushka.elcat.kg; http://www.adoptbabushka.org). For 150 euro annually, a low-income elderly person will receive a cash supplement of 10 euro a month (with 30 euro of the annual fee going toward operating expenses), a large help for people often living on pensions of 10-20 euro a month. The organization also provides a variety of support services to needy and lonely elderly. I verified that the money intended for my babushka reached her.

Community Based Tourism accepts volunteers in the field, as well a volunteers who can provide translation assistance remotely. Contact the head office in Bishkek (see Other Services) or see: http://www.cbtkyrgyzstan.kg/index.php?option=com_content&task=view&id=19&Itemid=36.

Other

There is a gingerbread-like Russian orthodox **church** at 25 Togolok Moldo (at intersection with Jibek Jolu prospektisi), followed by a teal-domed mosque a bit futher along on the right.

You can play paintball at **Combat** (ul. Armeiskaya, between Chui and Gorkovo, in the Bishkek-Nan building; Tel: 986170, 430326; combat@paintball.kg; www.paintball.kg). Entrance is 100 som, plus 3 som per paintball (about 50-100 per game).

You can visit the **workshop of a craftsman of classical musical instruments** by calling Turat Akunov at (0517) 32 81 61. Open for visitors daily at Vostok-5, Yerevanskaya Str. 47.

At the **official state flagpole**, in the city square, you can watch the changing of the guard, done hourly on the hour between 7 a.m. and 6 p.m.

One of the nicest aspects of Bishkek is the prevalence of parks. It has more trees per capita than any other Central Asian city. Two of the most pleasant places for people-watching and a stroll are: **Panfilov Park (behind the White house, it includes an amusement park, a ferris wheel, and tennis courts) and **Prospekt Erkindik** (between Prospekt Chui and the Railway station), where you can stroll across the city under a silver poplar awning and watch families enjoying the outdoors in all seasons.

If you'll be in town for a while, get on the email mailing list of the Swiss Agency for Development and Cooperation (SDC) by sending an email to: emilia.salieva@sdc.net; www.swisscoop.kg. SDC sends out announcements of interesting cultural events.

**Try to stop by the wedding palace (near Hyatt and the circus) on a Saturday or Sunday, especially after Ramadan, to see a parade of jubilant parties. Outside the building, limos and musicians offer their services.

Learn to ride a horse before you head out to the *jailoo* at the **Health Club** (147a Imanaliev str. Orto-Sai; Tel: 550378; cell: 0502 322-902; Tel/Fax: 55-08-06). For beginners, riding lessons cost 450 som/hour. If you can already ride, one hour costs 300 som. Riding lessons can be purchased in eight-lesson packages for a ten percent discount.

The **Mapleleaf Golf Course** (in Ortosai, near the Panorama café) charges 500 som for 9 holes, 100 som for clubs, 100 for caddy. The course is longer than most and generally well-kept, with great views of the foothills and occasional passing sheep or cows. The caddies, novice golfers themselves, have a good reputation. The burgers and fries are great and a clubhouse provides a place for a couple of beers after a round. Balls and tees are available for sale.

The Manas ayili complex (located just behind the Issyk-Kul Hotel. The hotel is on ul. Manas, 3 km past the U.S. embassy while heading out of Bishkek towards Ala-Archa) was built to celebrate 1,000 years of the Kyrgyz hero and epic Manas. Wedding parties frequently visit the complex to take pictures.

At the end of ul. Sovietskaya, on Yujnie Vorota (South Gates) is a park with a large monument to the victims of war.

Nightlife

For drinking, see **Metro Pub**, **Steinbrau**, **Fatboy's**, **TimeOut** and **Navigator** above.

For dancing, drinking and music, see **Cowboy Club**, **Stari Edgar** and **Apelsin** above.

The **Lounge Bar** (one floor above Fire and Ice on Derzhinskovo and Chui) serves drinks amidst sofas and relaxing music. In summer, seating is available on the terrace. There are also many places on Yujnie vorota (the southern gates of Bishkek).

Promzona (www.promzona.kg) – Live, rock music on the weekends and jazz nights on Tuesdays. It has a comfortable and relaxed atmosphere. It's location on the edge of the city makes it one of the more distant clubs, but a nice escape. Entrance 100-200 som depending on day of week.

The local expat community gathers first at **Metro Pub** (See Where to Eat), then heads to **Golden Bull** (Propekt Chui 209; Tel: 620131), the only place U.S. military are allowed to go. These are the English-speaking meat markets.

Popular **Nightclubs** include:

Retro Metro (Prospekt Mira 24; near intersection with ul. Gorkovo, across from old stadium Instrumentalnik; Tel: 541562; retro-metro@ yandex.ru; www.Retro-Metro.kg)

Ibiza (ul. Kulatova 91, near ul. Ibraimova, or ex-Pravda).

City (ul. Jukeeva-Pudovkina in the 8th microdistrict).

Rockbar Zepellin (next to TETs (central heating station) on the way to Alamedin).

Heaven (in the Dostuck Hotel on ul. Ibraimova (Pravda) and Frunze; on the 2nd floor).

Fire and Ice (ulitsa Derzhinsovo and Chui Prospect; Mon-Sun 9 p.m.-5 a.m.) is one of the most popular nightclubs where the singer Johnny frequently performs. Open from 10 p.m. to 6 a.m. daily.

Apple (ul. Manas and Moscovskaya) plays a lot of techno music.

Pharaoh (east side of the Philharmonic).

The **Ambassador disco** (Chui Prospekt, one kilometer east of TSUM) tends to attract fights.

There are several **casinos** in town. You can identify them by their neon lights. At the **XO casino** (ul. Frunze 338A) there is a bowling alley and lounge.

Transport

In town:

Taxis in Bishkek are reliable with drivers usually basing themselves on a certain corner, and other drivers there knowing him. For extra security, many radio-called taxi companies offer pick-up services. It's common for taxi drivers to offer you their cell phone number. You can call them directly for a pick-up.

The main local form of transport are *marshrutkis*, minibuses that hold about 14 passengers. You have to figure out which *marshrutka* goes where you are heading, then flag it down anywhere along its route. The fare is five som and they run from early morning until after 9 p.m. A helpful public transportation directory (*Spravochnik – Marshrutov Dvizheniya Obshestvennovo Transporta po goroda Bishkek*) is occasionally published and offered for sale. It's worth seeking out. Ask bus drivers or contact adani04@mail.ru, Tel: 43-22-30 or 0502-358510.

You can rent a bicycle from Red Fox (ul. Sovietskaya 65; near ul. Kulatova Tel: 544233, Fax: 544219; redfox@ak-sai.com) for 600 som/day.

Reliable drivers:

Almaz (0502 20 1842) – based near Moskovskaya and Pravda. Works from 9-10 a.m. to 10 p.m.

Almaz (Tel: 0502 344235; based near Bokonbaevo and Logvinenko) is a reliable driver who offers fair prices.

Fourteen taxi service companies compete with each other as well as the independent cars throughout the city. **Super-Taksi** (Tel: 152 or 29-56-69; supertaxi152@netmail.kg) is a reliable taxi service. Fares are 75 within the city during the day, 100 at night, 350 to the airport, and 10 som/km outside of the city. Different size and makes of cars are available. **Express Taxi** (Tel: 156) is also popular. **Salam Taxi** (Tel: 188) offers the cheapest fares to the airport (300 som one-way, 450 round-trip) and consistent 70-som fares in the city (90 after 10 p.m.). **Evro Taxi** (Tel: 150) uses only Mercedes. **Udacha Taxi** (Tel: 154) offers 75-som night fares. And **Ekonomtaxi** (Tel: 906060) has the cheapest prices, with 60-som fares in the city, 80 som after 10 p.m. Like Salam, it travels to the airport for 300 som (400 roundtrip).

Out of Bishkek:

Sergey Uriev (Tel: 670591; mobile: 580484) has 6-17 seat minivans/minibuses available to travel anywhere in Kyrgyzstan. The service is especially useful for trips to the local ski bases – Orusai, Norus, Tugus Bulak, which run a reasonable 1500-1600 som.

Taxis in town are taken individually, but taxis going to other towns can either be hired individually or shared with four other passengers. Agree on the fare before departure.

Buses leaving town depart from the Eastern and Western bus stations. The Eastern bus station serves locations just beyond the eastern suburbs, such as **Kant, Tokmok** and **Issyk-Ata**. Most long-distance buses depart from the Western bus station (Tel: 65-42-69), including buses to **Issyk-Kul, Almaty** and **Kashgar**. To get there, take *marshrutka* 113 or 235 from the intersection of Chui Prospekt and Karpinskovo. At the Western station you can also catch a taxi directly to **Sary-Chelek**. Aijibek (Tel: 0502 518128) will make the round-trip for 4800 for the car or 600/person/each way. If you want to pay for the entire car, you can visit in advance and make arrangements with the driver to pick you up directly from your lodgings.

Trains are mostly used for Bishkek to **Moscow** service, which takes three days. Slow routes go to **Novosibirsk** and **Novokuznetsk** in Siberia via **Almaty** and the Turksib route goes to **Yekaterinburg**, Russia via **Astana**.

Shared taxis to **Talas** are located inside the western station, to the left of the building as facing it. Drivers charge 400 som per passenger, 450 to be dropped off at destination. There are two routes to Talas from Bishkek. A paved road runs via Kazakhstan (400 kilometers or 250 miles), but you need a Kazakh visia. Most travel through Kyrgyzstan (300 kilometers or 185 miles), over two mountains. The trip takes five to six hours. To order a taxi to or from Talas, try: Nurland (careful driver with Audi 100 and seatbelts that function, even in back, Chingis, Talant (Tel: 0502 731992) or Baktigul (Tel: 0502 430717).

10-15 *marshrutkis* run daily between Bishkek and **Talas**, charging 300 som per person and taking 5-5.5 hours.

A minibus to **Tamchy** costs 150 som (3 hours); to **Cholpon-Ata**, 180 som. A shared taxi to Cholpon-Ata costs 400 som/person and takes 150 minutes. Official taxi services charge 2500 one way to Cholpon-Ata or 3200 round-trip. Expect prices to increase 30-50% in summer.

Shared taxis to **Bokonbaevo** leave from the Zapadni station and cost 250 som/person. Most leave between 10 and 11 a.m. A seat in a marshrutka costs 180 som.

A taxi to **Balikchy** costs 250 som/person and takes 1.5-2 hours. An official taxi service would charge 2000 som. A minibus costs 130 som and takes two hours. Expect prices to increase in summer.

A minibus to **Karakol** costs 250 som and takes about four hours.

Buses to **Kok Sai**, in the Talas region, leave from the Western bus station at 8 a.m.

A taxi from Bishkek to **Naryn** takes six hours and costs around 450 som. In the summer, taxis depart through the evening.

Prices to **Issyk-Kul** rise considerably (20-25% in summer). Most vehicles to the south shore leave in the morning. A taxi to **Karakol** or **Tyup** costs 500-700 (depending on season) som per passenger (times 4 for the car) and takes about five hours. To Cholpon-Ata, a seat costs 300-400 som and the trip takes about four hours.

Between four and seven flights per day travel between Bishkek and **Osh. The one-hour flight is a spectacularly beautiful journey over snowy mountain peaks towering over clouds. With one-way tickets from $68, it's worth the trip just for the scenery. Check-in about 40 minutes before your flight. The flight is about 50 minutes. Buy tickets at Kyrgyz Concept, other travel agencies, or directly at the airport. For updated schedules, check http://eng.concept. kg/OshConcept/schedule. Taxis and marshrutkis cover the 730 kilometers (455 miles) in 10 or more hours. It is one of the most beautiful drives you'll take in your life. Spend the extra money for a taxi so that you can stop and take some pictures. Shared taxis start at 1200 som/person, *marshrutkis* from 1000 som.

Other Services

Internet

   Internet Cafes are located throughout town. Choices include: the **post office** (corner of Chui Prospekt and Sovietskaya; last counter on right inside; 30 som/hour; good connection; open 7 a.m. to 8 p.m., Sundays 8 .m. to 7 p.m.); **Soyuz** (intersection of Pravda and Moskovskaya streets, open 24 hours, rate based on traffic, about 70 som/hour, speed is good, but can't connect laptops to internet here and it's expensive compared to other places); **Valley Net** (corner of Kiev and Manas; 35 som/hour; good connection); **Internet Club Kami** (34 Manas), 30 som/hour, open 24 hours; **Park Net Internet Club** (Chui 134; 45/hour plus traffic; open 9 to midnight). **Sirius Internet Club** (on Soviet and Chui, across from post office and telecom) has good connections, including pdf, flash card and IP telefonica; 40 som/hour.

Salons and spas

Territoria Spa (ul. Moskovskaya 184; Tel: 664114; 210766 (nail bar), 662434 (office); Vefa Center, ul. Gorkovo 90; Tel: 596461, 596460, 596490) is a first-class spa, frequented by foreigners and upper class Bishkek women. Modern, comfortable and customer-friendly, it offers top quality services – sauna, hydro-massage, massages, manicures, pedicures, hair, fitness (1500 som for 12 classes/month, or 250 per class), including a wonderful spa day – a full day of luxury for 3,000 som. **Prestige Image Salon (on ul. Kievskaya, between Togolok Moldo and the street towards Tsum) (500 for pedicure, 500 for massage) is also recommended. **Adam and Eve** beauty and health salon (ul. Moskovskaya 217, on corner of Kalyk Akieva; Tel: 650288; open from 9-9 daily) offers massages.

Sharm (ul. Kievskaya 88/Erkindik 43, near intersection with Derzhinskovo/Erkindik; Tel: 662222; 666737; Open 8-8) is a high quality salon, offering haircuts for 250, manicures for 150 and massages (Ulan is great) from 200-400 som. Other recommended places for a haircut include **Valeri (across from Narodni on ul. Toktogul and Kalyk Akieva) and **Rosphor** (on Ahunbayeva).

Shopping

The **Vefa complex**, on ul. Sovietskaya and Gorkovo (ul. Gorkovo 21/1), is Bishkek's first shopping mall, opened in 2006 – with a Turkish-oriented food court on the top floor, a modern theater (tickets 100-150 som), Ramstore supermarket and a variety of high-end shopping, including books, sporting equipment, Gap, Benetton, Levis and Ecco. Free parking available in underground lot.

The Places of Kyrgyzstan – Bishkek

I felt at home in my neighborhood, comfortably leaving and entering at all times of the day and night. The young boys greeted me as if I were a neighborhood fixture. Old women sat on benches, wearing thick socks and scarves around their heads, talking or people-watching for hours at a time. Families walked across a busy street – some patriarchs wore tall, white felt kalpaks, some religious women from the nearby *madrassa* donned headscarves, some young adults entered the nearby casino in the latest Western fashions.

On a beautiful fall day, the bright yellow and crinkled brown leaves fell like a constant, light rainshower. From the window of my apartment, I watched children in mismatched clothing playing on the slide. It was the one toy not taken apart by people who stole metal to resell to China. The children would bunch together at the bottom of the slide, hitting one another like carts of a train joining together, laughing hysterically at the pretended accidental crash.

In the afternoon, I went to meet my friend at Vefa, Bishkek's first modern shopping center. Vika's son Bagdan loved the transparent elevator and Vika marveled at the lights that hung three stories down from the ceiling.

Vefa features a children's play area on the top floor, which charges an unbeatable 50 cents per hour. There is a movie theater (playing cheap, second-run Western movies) and a fast food court. But the fast food doesn't include any Western giants. Instead, it smells of *kebab*. Most of the stands have a Turkish influence and several sell English tea in glazed ceramic Turkish mugs.

The local population seems to have embraced it. Like shopping malls that attract teenagers hanging out in the West, Vefa provides a place for local youth and adults to casually meet and see something new.

On my way home, I stopped when I saw two soldiers in the road, holding glow-in-the-dark red batons. They stopped traffic to allow a company of troops to cross the street. The soldiers came out of one building, in formation, dressed in green khaki, and proudly singing a song in Kyrgyz. They marched into the other building, still singing. I knew my friend's brother served there – that the soldiers are mostly kids for whom studies didn't work out. But it was nice to see them proud and professional, even when crossing a street in the dark of night.

You can find just about anything you need, from toilet paper to a cell phone at **TSUM** (Chui Prospekt, between Pravda and Sovietskaya). The fourth floor has a particularly good selection of souvenirs. They also have several clothing repair booths, on the first and third floors. **U Zhanni** (first floor, on the right; Tel: 0502-33-21-10) does quick alterations for about $3-10 per article.

Some of the best cakes in Bishkek can be found at **Magnolia** (ul. Manas, near the intersection with Moskovsakaya).

For books, the best selection of English-language books is found at **Metro Pub** (see Where to Eat).

Need an evening gown quick? One place to try is **Butik A-15** at Dordoi Plaza. Most run about $100-150.

You can find maternity clothes at **Milaya Mama** (Caravan Shopping Center, ul. Kievskaya 128; 3rd floor, boutique D-23; Tel: 909400).

If you are looking to buy a car, head to the **Azabat Avtorinok** (also called Kudai Bergin), a short ride from Shlagbau (you can get to Shlagbau by taking marshrutka 216 west from Tsum. There may be marshrutkis that go directly to the car market). The packed market, open on Saturdays and Sundays, includes not only local cars, but cars brought in from the Baltics.

There is a Chinese products store at the intersection of ulitsas Sovietskaya and Jibek Jolu.

You can find a good selection of videos and CDs at **Meloman** (ul. Frunze 340; at intersection with Sovietskaya; Tel: 623993; 596474; 906280)

Souvenirs (usually will only negotiate down 5%):
Tumar art salon (136 Chui Prospek; Tel: 667368, fax: 212653; tumar@tumar.com; www.tumar.com; open 10-7) is a favorite for quality products in colors and styles favored by foreign visitors.

Casca (on Togolok Moldo, between Kiev and Moscovskaya, down a small driveway in between two apartment buidings) is an NGO where all money earned from sales goes to local artisans. Known to have reasonable prices.

Asahi (Асахи) Handicrafts (136 Chui; Tel/Fax: 665710; info@ asahikyrgyz.com; Open 9-8) has a nice selection of pricy, but good-quality crafts, as well as some antique dishes and farm tools. It's located next to an Italian restaurant, across the street from Park Net, on Chui Prospect.

Other places to try include: **Kiyal** (202 Chui, Osh market Kiyal factory; Tel: 651442, 242878; Open 9-5), **Belek** (Chui Prospekt, Ilbirs industrial complex building, ground floor; Tel: 661302; Open 9-6), and **Saimaluu-Tash** (78 Pushkina, Ala-Too square; Tel: 620413; Open 10-6).

Instruction

You can study a variety of foreign languages in Bishkek, usually at reasonable prices. Russian and Kyrgyz language courses for foreigners are available from the **Congress of Women of Kyrgyzstan** (120 ul. Bokonbaevo; Tel: 66 45 49 or 66 42 13). The **London School** (39 ul. Sovietskaya, near the Vefa center; bishkekschool@gmail.com; http://www.tlsbi.com/index.html) offers intensive Russian and Kyrgyz classes. **Perspektiva Educational Center** (ul. Sovietskaya 170, 2nd floor, room 60; Tel: 663994) offers classes in English, Russian, Arabic, Turkish and Chinese.

Sports and fitness

Red Fox (ul. Baitik-Baatira 65 (on corner of ulitsa Kulatova (Sovietskaya)); Tel: 54-42-33; fax: 54-42-19; redfox@ak-sai.com) sells a variety of high quality outdoor and sporting gear. **Sportmaster** (Vefa Center, 3rd floor); Tel: 596666, 596565, 976666, 0502 325245) has a complete selection of sporting goods. **Extreme Plus** (ul. Gorkovo 41; Tel: 296783) also sells sports equipment. You can check out the ads for used equipment at diesel.elcat.kg (requires registration).

**KarVen Club (77 ulitsa Gogol; intersection of ulitsas Toktogul and Gogol; Tel: 68-06-96; 68-12-18; 68-08-20) is the one of the best places in town to work-out, with a nice, long outdoor pool (heated in winter), tennis courts, and a basic fitness center. Swimming costs 250 som per swim, aqua and standard aerobics run from 100-150 som, tennis is 300 som/hour, a trainer 480/hour, and massages run from 350-500 som. Monthly packages are available for a small savings.

**Reebok Club (ulitsa Sovietskaya 204 (near intersection with Frunze); Tel: 626868, 681012 and ultisa Gogolya 120; Tel: 627913; aerobics_center@mail.ru) is a friendly, good-value club, offering a full schedule of aerobics, yoga, belly-dancing, and latin dance classes (for 800-900 som/month or 100 som per class) and massage. Individual lessons available for 400-500 som/hour. Recommended.

Fitness Club Olympus at the Hyatt (ulitsa Sovietskaya 19, near the Opera and Ballet Theater; Tel: 661234; www.bishkek.hyatt.com) is the most elite club in town. Membership ranges from 1900 som for the day to 10,000 for a month, 26,250 for 3 months, or 75,000 for a year. This includes the training room, spa, Jacuzzi and outdoor pool.

Or visit between 10 and 4 for a 650 som day pass. Open from 6 a.m. to 10 p.m. daily.

Aerobics classes are also available from the **Women's Fitness Club** (Zhenski Fitness Klub), on Karpinskaya 14 (Tel: 28-56-82), in the old *dietski sad*. Classes are held three times a week and cost 100 som per visit or 500 per month.

Sharm Club Image Center (Bulvar Erkindik 42; Tel: 664597) offers fitness classes for 135 som per class (10% discount on monthly pass), as well as beauty services.

Mir Fitnesa (ul. Kievskaya 77; Fabrika Ilbirs, 4th floor, entrance on fountain side; Tel: 902750) offers shaping, dance and fitness classes.

Beli Parus, near the Medina market, has 2 pools and a kiddie area for swimming. It costs 300 som for a 24-hour pass.

There are old, cheap tennis courts on Sovietskaya and Donetskaya, near the 3rd children's hospital. 50 som/hour.

The **Sun Club** (2/1 Jukeev-Pudovkina Street – Off Ibraimov Street, between Kulatov and Lev Tolstoy, across from the Uchkun building; Tel: 44-16-16; www.sun-club.kg), opened in 2005, is a modern health and fitness club, including aerobics, up-to-date fitness equipment, and tae kwan do classes. Open 9 a.m. to 9 p.m. A one year membership for two (including free drinks and a free massage per month) costs $2400, a 4-person family membership $150/month, individual monthly memberships (for one activity) from $30-120/month. Individual visits are available to the training room ($8), shaping ($6), tae kwan do ($4), table tennis ($3) and massage ($10).

You can play tennis on clay courts in the center for Bishkek for 150 som/hour. Located between the café TimeOut and the rides in the park behind the White House, you can just show up or call **The Association of Tennis Enthusiasts** (ul. Kulatova 1a; Tel: 610829; mobile: (0502) 267695) ahead to make reservations. Rackets are available for rental.

Oleg Yuganov (ul. Firova 14a; Tel: 67-09-74; mobile: 0517 752346) runs a foreign-bike repair business from his home and also sells new and used bikes of good quality. To get there, go north on ul. Togolok Moldo (past the Russian church). Continue a few blocks past Jibek Jolu. Take a right on ul. Koronkaeva, immediately before Café Oke. Firova is the first street to the left. **Anton** (Tel: 0543 912060) is the Giant bike dealer for Kyrgyzstan. You can buy a good quality bike for around 7,000 som at **Sports Place**, at the intersection of ulitsas Moskovski and Turuzbekova.

One of the best ways to get out into the mountains surrounding Bishkek is to join one of the excursions organized every Sunday (year-round) by **Mikhail Mikhailovich Mikhailov** (Tel: 0772530438; 666-939; home tel: 292-985). A university professor of tourism and long-time physical education teacher, he has an amazing knowledge of and love for the outdoors. Every Sunday morning, a large group of local hiking or skiing enthusiasts meet at a corner downtown (usually Sovietskaya and Toktogul) and travel by bus to the day's destination. The prices vary based on the destination (some possibilities include Issyk-Ata, Belogorodka, Kultor, Kegeti and the canyons), but are commonly in the range of 120 to 160 som, including transportation and a guided hike by Mikhail. People bring picnic lunches. Call ahead (in Russian) to find out about upcoming trips and to reserve a seat.

Snow Land (10 microrayon, supermarket Narodnyi,; Tel: 697381) rents a good selection of skis, snowboards and sleds at competitive prices. They also sell new equipment. Conveniently located on the way out of town toward the ski slopes.

The best place for maps, both city and trekking, is **Geoid** (ul. Kievskaya 107-4; Tel: 21-22-02).

Travel

The corner of Toktogul and Tynestanova is the airline office corner, where you can find representatives of British Airlines, KLM, Carlsson Wagon Lit, Glavtour, Aeroflot, Lufthansa and Uzbek airlines.

ITC Asia Mountains Agency (1a ul. Lineinaja; aljona@mail. elcat.kg; asiamountains@mail.ru; http://www.asiamountains.co.uk/; Tel: 694073; 694075) offers travel services locally and throughout Kyrgyzstan. A one-day guided trip to the nearby Ala-Too mountains, including transportation and lunch, is $80 for one person, less per person for larger groups. They also offer private plane rental for $500/hour.

The **Celestial Mountains Tour Company** (ul. Kievskaya 131-2; Tel: 21-25-62; Fax: 61-0402; celest@infotel.kg) offers a variety of tours.

Ultimate Adventure (185 ul. Kurienkeva; Tel: 270754 (06 62 11 70 82 in France); ultiadv@mail.kg, Stephanie.aubree@wanadoo.fr; http://www.kirghizie.fr) organizes discovery, cultural and adventure tours. They work together with Babushka Adoption to orgainize visits for sponsors with their babushkas and dedushkas.

Kyrgyz Community Based Tourism Association (58 ulitsa Gorkovo (intersection with Matrossov); Tel/Fax: 559331; marketing@

cbtkyrgyzstan.kg, reservation@cbtkyrgyzstan.kg, cbttours@mail.ru, arajiev@yahoo.com; www.cbtkyrgyzstan.kg (local branch contacts available online); Open Monday-Friday 9-5). Started in 2000 by villagers in Kochkor; now 17 local CBT organizations exist, with more than 300 members throughout Kyrgyzstan. The association focuses on the best attractions in each region, with a good balance between quality and reasonable prices, as well as providing tourism work for locals. Currently CBT has offices in Bishkek, Arsalanbob, Bokonbaevo, Jalalabat, Kazarman, Karakol, Kara-Suu, Kochkor, Kyzyl-Oi, Naryn, Osh, Talas, Tamchy, Batken, Kerben, Alay, Sary-Mogul and Chon-Kemin. CBT partners with **Shepherd's Life**, a community based tourism group in Naryn.

Kyrgyz Concept (four locations in Bishkek: 100 ul. Razzakov Tel: 661331; Fax: 660220; office@concept.kg; 126 Chui prospect; Tel: 666006; Fax: 661011; aero2@concept.kg; 69 ul. Kievskaya Tel/Fax: 900404; aero3@concept.kg; 231 ul. Tynystanov Tel: 900866; Fax: 901241; aero5@concept.kg; http://eng.concept.kg/news/) is reliable and offers a full range of services, including air tickets, hotel reservations, event planning, transportation, visas, language courses and silk road tours.

Kyrgyz Travel Tourist Company (ul. Elebesov 237; Tel: 670764, 679975; Fax: 670764; d-sasha@elcat.kg; http://kyrgyz-travel.com), a friendly company owned by an alpinist and a chef, offers a variety of hiking, horseback riding, and mountain-biking tours. Their focus is on the mountains along the southern shore of lake Issyk-Kul. They also own a guesthouse in Tamga (see where to stay in Tamga).

The **Edelweiss Travel Company** (ul. Usenbaeva 68/9; Tel: 280788, 284254; Fax: 680038; edelweiss@elcat.kg; http://www.edelweiss.elcat. kg/) offers trekking, helicopter skiing, mountaineering, horseback riding and auto safari tours.

Silk Road Water Center (Tel: 0517 75-09-72; Kyrgyzraft@mail. ru; www.rafting.com.kg) offers professional rafting and fishing trips, with an emphasis on safety. Raft on one of several rivers, of varying levels (2-6) and lengths. Three of the rivers flow from the Tien Shan glaciers. A highly recommended experience.

Carlson Wagonlit Travel (93 ultitsa Toktogula; Tel: 666102/666052; Fax: 663850; also office at Manas airport, 3rd floor; Tel: 693040; 693090; Fax: 693090; airport@swtrep.kg) is a reliable agency, especially for international flights.

Dostuck-Trekking (18th Linea St., 42-1; Tel: 545455; 427471, 540237; Fax: 545455, 559090; dostuck@saimanet.kg; www.dostuck.

com.kg) offers a variety of tours and activities, including whitewater rafting. They specialize in hiking and climbing trips.

Nomads Land (50 ul. Mederova; Tel: 936-479; 0502 446666; info@nomadsland.kg; www.nomadsland.kg) also specializes in active and adventure tours such as biking, hiking, rafting and horseback riding, with a focus on supporting and involving the local community.

Community Based Tourism

Community Based Tourism (CBT) is Kyrgyzstan's premier service matching tourists with local guesthouses, guides and drivers and is a model of successful community tourist development.

Started in 2000 and registered in January, 2003, the organization works to improve living conditions in remote regions by using local natural and recreational resources. It strives to preserve the area's culture and resources while also teaching service providers how to provide the comfort tourists desire. Currently, the association unites 17 communities plus Shepherd's Life, a 5-group association of shepherd families offering *jailoo*, or yurt, tourism.

The number of tourists using CBT services has increased from 4,860 in 2004 to 7,747 in 2007. Currently 381 families earn income through the provision of CBT services. In addition to its regular menu of tourist services, CBT also organizes an annual ecological clean-up near Son-Kul Lake, uniting both tourists and locals in the event. In addition, it sponsors occasional special trips to see horse races, craft festivals and other events.

Booking a stay or a visit through CBT is a good way to know you will be benefiting the local communities while receiving reliable services.

Services

Novost drycleaners (Moskovskaya 2, near ul. Karpinskovo) works daily from 8-6. They take 2-3 days to clean. However, they don't sew, and may require you to take off buttons or other adjustments that will require work after receiving the goods back. There is a **drycleaners** in the Asia Store on Chui Prospect, to the right of the United Nations building.

The best rates for **exchanging money** (dollars, euros and rubles are taken most easily, as are Kazakh tenge and Chinese yuan) is at the exchange booths. The exchange center is located at Moscovskaya and

Sovietskaya streets. Most are good, but count your money carefully, and beware of places that offer you a large pile of small bills. They are most likely to be cheating. The one to the right of Farad Tserokopii (фарад церокопии) is especially egregious. Banks have a slightly lower rate, but are reliable. The best time to exchange money is from 10 to 5 on weekdays. At other times, the rate goes down slightly.

Several banks offer **cash advances** on Visa/Mastercard, including Demir Kyrgyz Bank, Kazkomerzbank and Halyk Bank. Many banks also have Western Union **money transfer** services. You can find **ATMs** at Beta Stores and Narodni as well as Kazkommerzbank, Demir Bank and Halyk Bank. These generally charge $3 and allow you to take out $300 per day. At the Hyatt, you can remove as much as you want, with a fee that goes up along with the sum.

You can get **passport photos** (4 for 100 som) at ProPhoto (Chui Prospekt), in the Fabrika Ilbiks building on the central square, just past the fountain.

If you need your digital camera repaired, you can find a repair shop at ul. Kievkaya 104 (Tel: 627255; Open Monday-Friday 9-5, Saturday 9-2). It's near the back side of the central square, across from the bus stop, on the 2nd floor of the Dom Bwita.

There is an **international church**, at the United Bible Seminary on the NW corner of Jibek Jbolu and Isanova. Services are in English at 10 a.m. and 5 p.m.

You can buy stamps, cards, and envelopes, use internet, and ship packages at the **post office**. To ship packages, go in the door to the left of the main entrance. Once you've entered and walked down the hallway, the door on the right is for mailing books, the door straight ahead is for packages. To send a package, you'll have to fill out four forms, then a customs form, then write the name and address one more time on the package. Bring a box or a plastic bag if you have it, but don't seal it before coming. Air mail to the U.S. takes 2-4 weeks, surface mail up to two months. Open 7-8, Sunday and holidays 8-7.

You can call the U.S. for five som per minute at **Alfa (Алфа)** (ulitsas Sovietskaya and Toktogul). Many internet cafes offer IP-telephony, the ability to make low-cost calls through the internet.

Professional Services

The most reputable law firms in Bishkek include **Kalikova**, **Partner**, and **Diamond**.

SIAR Research and Consulting (164a Chui #409; Tel: 663637, 210925; Fax: 663636; ainouras@siar-consult.com; www.siar-consult.com) provides high-quality survey research services.

The Traditions of Kyrgyzstan – Nooruz

Nooruz is a shamanistic rite celebrated throughout Central Asia. It marks the beginning of spring and is an Islamic adaptation of the shamanist vernal equinox or renewal celebrations. Often banned in Soviet times, it became an official Soviet celebration in 1989, a concession hoped to distract attention from Muslim nationalism.

On this day, people celebrating at home have a special meal that should include separate, symbolic items for men and women as well as seven items that being with "sh" in Kyrgyz: wine, milk, sweets, sugar, a peanut sweet, candle and a bud. It's marked by festivities on Bishkek's central square and horse races in Talas and elsewhere.

On this day, I walked with my friend Zhenya, a saleswoman who enjoyed mountain hiking in her spare time, down Bishkek's main street, Chui Prospect. Already at Tsum, the central department store, the streets filled with people. Outside Tsum, a crowd formed a semi-circle around a woman playing a traditional instrument, the high-pitched, haunting strains floating in the air.

As we walked farther into town, closer to the central square and the White House, the crowds thickened.

"Russians usually stay home on this day," Zhenya said. "The Kyrgyz all come from the villages, together with their children. The Russians are afraid because the Kyrgyz get wild. Especially at night, when they get drunk."

Herself a mix of nationalities, Zhenya considered herself Russian. As she said, there were very few non-Kyrgyz outside. But except for throwing their garbage wherever they happened to sit, the people we saw were very well-behaved. A festive spirit ran through the air, with small children running ahead of their parents, squealing with delight.

"Do you notice how many small children there are?" Zhenya asked. "Even in these times, when everything is unstable, people continue to have kids."

The central square was decorated with a large concert stage, giant banners announcing Nooruz 2006 and Kyrgyz flags. Photographers worked feverishly, earning money selling their services to the crowds. All along the road we passed stuffed elephants and tigers, plastic chairs and plastic flowers, felt covered boards announcing Nooruz, flowers and balloons, all intended as backgrounds for Polaroid photos.

Zhenya spoke of a friend of hers who had moved to Almaty and missed Bishkek. "The people here are so much simpler than in Kazakhstan," Zhenya said. "You'd never see things like those dirty plastic chairs that people here are willing to pay to be photographed on."

For the rest of the day, she made a point of exposing all the things that would only happen in Kyrgyzstan. Many of them – like the cheap games of luck people thought up to make money, and the people sitting and eating in the grass – didn't phase me at all. I wouldn't have paid any special notice.

But others were definitely unique to Kyrgyzstan. "Look at those people gathering used glass bottles, right in front of the White House," she said, laughing. And she was right. Just a few feet away from the most powerful office in the country, people collected and lined up brown, green and white bottles to sell.

We walked along the art gallery row, where vendors sell paintings under awnings. We watched people playing a game throwing large bones (from which animal, no one seemed to know) into the center of a circle. The willow trees hung in green threads and the small apricots already bloomed pink. We heard the sound of popping balloons, of laughing children, and smelled all the national dishes offered for sale – various animal innards, steamed meat-filled dumplings, fried rice with carrot and beef, meat kebabs, and the special holiday treat – *sumalak* – a brown sweet made from wheat germ and sold in small plastic cups. A friend from Osh had told me about it – how difficult it is to make, how long it takes, how it's only made for Nooruz. Only women can make it and the many steps include soaking the wheat for three days until it sprouts, grinding it, mixing it with oil, sugar and flour, and cooking it for 24 hours. So I had to try it. But *sumalak* tasted grainy, not as good or as sweet as she'd led me to expect.

"They probably have one version they make at home and another version for sale," Zhenya explained.

A bicycle taxi pedaled past us, on the street closed to traffic, and huge stands of balloons puffed up with offerings of Ronald McDonald, Spiderman and Donald Duck.

Our final stop was the ferris wheel. Zhenya was reluctant to stand in line, but I convinced her it would be worth it. It was a slow, steadily moving wheel, with red, blue, green and yellow carriages that seated four people each. We paid and climbed aboard, sitting atop the hard, metal seats.

As we rose, we could see all the festivities going on below – the children twirling around on the rusting rides, the families seated in the grass, the activities on the central square, the golden domes of a central square building. Even from a distance we could hear the high-pitched laughter.

We could see a carpet of violets abloom under white-trunked trees. "Spring is really here," Zhenya said. By participating in Nooruz, we'd officially marked it.

Excursions from Bishkek

**Ata-Beyit (Ата Бейит), 25 kilometers (15 miles) from Bishkek, serves the joint purpose of a military base and a memorial for people shot as enemies of the people during Stalin's rule. On the night of November 5 and 6, 1938, 138 bodies of people who had been shot in Bishkek basements were brought to a mass grave here. Victims included Turukul Aitmatov (the father of Chingis Aitmatov) and Zhupov Abdurahmanov, the first representative of the Soviet party in Kyrgyzstan. At the time, this was a KGB rest zone. Under cover of night, the perpetrators thought no one saw the burial. But a warehouse worker at the base witnessed it. Before he died, he told his daughter, then aged 11, that something bad happened there. He told her to tell people about it when the time was right. In 1991, she came forward. Here, in the memorial and museum constructed in 2000, you can see the site, a former brick oven, where the bodies were found, and learn about the Stalinist repression of 40,000 residents of Kyrgyzstan. On November 8th, relatives of the dead gather annually for a memorial. The museum is open daily but Monday, admission 10 som. Accessible by marshrutka 295 or by taxi.

There are some nice hiking opportunities near the village of **Sasnovka**, about 100 kilometers (62 miles) west of Bishkek. To get there, take marshrutka 216 west from Tsum to Shlagbau, then take a minibus towards Karabalta or a taxi (250 som). Shortly past the toll booth, on the left, is *Zona Otdiha Sharki Ratma* (Зона отдыха шаркы ратма). Look for the exit immediately before the bridge, where a faded white sign with green letters stands. A ten-minute hike up a path will bring you to a waterfall. There are several fire pits along the river, but the area is overused and doesn't feel tranquil. A bit further down the main road, at the river Turuk, a waterfall is visible on the right. A path up the left side of the waterfall is a great one to follow for a day hike. Bring a picnic lunch.

Issyk-Ata is a former Soviet resort and a popular place for relaxation and hiking. For lodging, your best bet is to knock on any door in the apartment blocks just outside of the *kurort* (resort). Most townspeople make their living renting out rooms to tourists and you should easily find a room. It runs about 80 som/person/night. Since locals have a hard time getting into the city, they also appreciate contributions of groceries. To get there, you can take a local bus from the Eastern bus station (call for schedule), hire a taxi from **Kant** (a city of 25,000 on the edge of Bishkek and home to Kyrgyzstan's first sugar industry – many *marshrutkis* run between Bishkek and Kant), or hitchhike from **Krasnaya Rechka**. Start a visit to Issyk-Ata by walking through the decaying resort and past the Lenin statue. Walk through the turnstile and follow the path to the waterfall. About two hours futher on is a second waterfall. Behind that mountain are three small but picturesque lakes. Horses may be available for hire along the trails. The perfect end to a hike is a dip in the **thermal spring**, just above the apartment buildings. Natural warm water emerges from the mountain through pipes and into two pools, steaming with the warmth. The small pool has pipes that gush water onto your back, giving you a massage. The large pool is good for swimming. Entrance costs 20 som for the large pool or 40 som for the small pool (with spigots for hydro-massage). It's open from 8 to 6 year-round. Bathing in the warm waters on a cool day and peering through the steam at the surrounding mountains is definitely one of the highlights of a visit to Kyrgyzstan. It's good to bring some picnic food, or groceries for a long visit. Small cafes sell hot food and drinks and in the summer, mare's milk is available along the trail.

The Places of Kyrgyzstan – Issyk-Ata

Our hiking group piled into an old green and white bus with green hubcaps. It started with a bang and we took off on our way to Issyk-Ata, a sanatorium an hour and 20 minutes from Bishkek.

The passengers wore Russian sports suits in teal, fuchsia and navy, wool caps, sweaters and several carried walking sticks. The bus traversed the flat, tree-lined road toward the mountains, moving smoothly on the asphalt and bouncing on the potholed rural roads. As we passed village after village, the residents stopped what they were doing to watch us pass by, as though it were the most interesting thing they'd seen all day.

My attention wavered between watching the scrub-filled land turn a hesitant green and looking at a screen at the front of the bus, where our leader Mikhail showed videos of previous hikes – filled with waterfalls, flowers, canyons and mountains. Several people had picked up hot, fresh *lepushkas* (round, flat loaves of white bread) at our stop in a dusty village. Steam rose from my seatmate's *lepushka* like a gaseous sun. I could almost taste the soft, sweet yeastiness.

We disembarked at the entrance to the sanatorium. I was a regular on Mikhail's hiking trips and usually I took the long, challenging route he offered. But this time, due to snow, even at low levels, we couldn't take our usual long hike. The snow deepened quickly and we didn't have the boots or the time needed to plod through it. Since we couldn't hike as far as usual, we were able to move at a slower pace, to be more like tourists rather than athletes for once.

We moved through the sanatorium facilities towards the park beyond its gates. Once a popular rest area, the white buildings had fallen into disrepair and it was no longer open to the public.

On a hillside not far from the sanatorium, Mikhail showed us a rock with a smooth, cold depression. If you put your bare leg into it, he said, you'd be guaranteed either a wedding or the birth of a child within a year. True to form, I got engaged seven months later and married in just under one year.

From there, we moved to a Buddhist rock that Mikhail told us was holy and emanates energy. A carving of Buddha in the lotus position and a Tibetan text were covered in bronze.

"This is from the 2nd century and it's still here," Mikhail told us, pointing at the Buddha. A carving of Lenin on the opposite side of the rock, done within the past few decades, had almost been erased by the elements. He implied that the poor quality of Communist art did not compare with ancient religious work.

We walked a little further to a cobblestone staircase that led to the curative waters the sanatorium guests used to visit. Although it smelled like rotten eggs, we drank it for the benefit of our health. At a pool famed for its curative powers on the eyes, my fellow passengers splashed their eyes with water.

Our next stop was a snowy path that led to a hidden waterfall in the mountains. Much of the water had frozen on the way down, forming an ice cave through which the rest of the water flowed.

For a dollar each, we got a relaxing swim in the thermal pools. The 125-degree water comes out right from the mountains into the swimming pool. The changing rooms were outdoors, basic stalls to the side of the pools. This made for a frigid entry and exit, stripping down and changing into a suit in the winter air, and even worse, pulling off the wet suit and trying to dry off afterwards.

Nevertheless, the experience of jumping into the steaming waters on a cool day, vibrating as the massaging waters pour out of tubes onto your back, and looking up and out at snow-peaked mountains and a wide, wild sky made it worth it.

Tuyug Issak-Ata is a canyon near Issyk-Ata – a nice place for a cool, moderate walk through a forest, leading into the **Kok mainok canyon**, which used to be an alpinist base in Soviet times. At the gate where the path forks, you'll find a mineral spring over a fence. Go through the gate to fill your bottles. To reach a series of small ponds, follow the fence to the right. In summer, beekeepers sell fresh honey from the hives at the entrance to the canyon.

Whitewater rafting trips (one day and longer) are available on the Chui and Chon Kemin rivers. The Chon Kemin trip starts in the Chon Kemin national park. Check out www.rafting.com.kg.

****Keltor** (which means "place of lakes") is located 85 km (53 miles) from Bishkek. Fresh honey is offered for sale at the base. A 3.5-4 hour, 22 kilometer (13.5 mile) hike leads to a beautiful alpine lake at 2900 meters (9,514 feet). There are two places to stay nearby. The **Edelweis** hotel, a former camp, has clean sheets and charges 120 som/night. You must bring your own food. The **Aksuu Sanatorium** is an acceptable place, charging 130 som/night with meals.

Kegeti is the sight of a popular waterfall. A three-hour hike will take you to a more pristine and less visited area and a second waterfall.

**The Suluterek canyons, enroute to Issyk-Kul (about 1.5 hours (135 km or 84 miles) from Bishkek) are a nice place for a hike, especially in fall. The temperature in the mountain-enclosed area is usually 5-10 degrees Celsius higher than outside. Best to visit with a guide or group (see Mihail Mihailovich's tours).

Mihail Mihailovich Mihailov (Tel: 0502 530438; vertikal45@ mail.ru) leads cheap and high-quality **tours to the areas outside of Bishkek every Sunday, year round. They attract mostly locals, plus foreigners in the know. He goes hiking in the summer and skiing in winter. Call before Sunday to sign up and he'll tell you the meeting place (usually Sovietskaya and Toktogul) and time (usually between 8 and 9 a.m.). Trips usually cost around 150 som for transport. Bring your own lunch.

**Skiing: With several bases within 90 minutes of Bishkek and lift tickets well under $10 a day, Kyrgyzstan is an excellent place for anyone with an interest in skiing to get some practice on the slopes. Bases generally operate from early January through March or early April.

Some of the most popular ski bases include:

Kashka-Suu Ski Resort (Tel: (3312) 064-506 or 434-835 or 211-141) is located at 1700 meters (5,577 feet), about an hour outside

Bishkek, on a rough, uphill road. Accommodation in chilly dormitory style chalets with no hot water costs 350 night, food is 400 som per day. A heavy-duty vehicle runs like a bus in winter, taking passengers to the remote, beautiful mountain valley location. The base has a chairlift and a pull lift, as well as a small ice rink (bring your own skates or reserve your size ahead of time).

Norus (Tel/Fax: 0312 661111), located 38 kilometers (24 miles) from Bishkek, is one of the easiest bases to visit for a day trip. Or if you prefer to make a weekend out of it, a good quality hotel, **Hotel Rasputin** (Tel: 0502 335523; 0555 502696; hotel_rasputin@inbox. ru) is located on the ski base. The base has two pull lifts. Rent your skis or snowboard in Bishkek and bring them to the base.

Oruu-Sai (Tel: (0517) 75-32-38; (0312) 983239, 571985) is also within 40 kilometers (25 miles) of Bishkek. A hotel is available on premises with rooms from $30 to $45. Located at 2200 meters (7,218 feet), it has three drag lifts, equipment rental, lodging and a café.

Toguz Bulak (9 springs) (119 ul. Grazhdanskaya, room 19, Tel.: 0312 936479, 0517 757998, 0502 446666; http://www. toguz-bulak.webou.net/mainen.htm), with a 2500 meter (8,200 foot) chairlift, has the best chairlift available in the resorts near Bishkek. Located at 1900 meters (6,233 feet), it has ordered snow-making machines and is building a pool and cottages. A restaurant is available on-premises. But if you are not staying in the hotel, the staff expect you to go outside as soon as you finish eating, meaning you must leave your gear in the car or on an outside table. Individual cottages (for 2-5 people) cost $80-100/night. Hotel rooms cost 500 som per person. The base has two runs and horses available for rent. Ski and snowboard rental is also available for 600 som/day, but they sometimes run out of popular sizes. Instructors, snowmobiles and ATVs are also available. Chairlift tickets available on a daily (300 som) or per use (70 som) basis. One of the nine mineral springs is near the base of the resort. Ask staff how to get there to fill your water bottles.

Orlovka is located about 100 kilometers (62 miles) from Bishkek, on the way to Issyk-Kul. Since it has snow-making machines, this is the place to go if snowcover is light. The base has three pull lifts. Equipment is available for rent and ski instruction is available. Hotel and sauna on premises.

A new ski base has opened in **Tuya-Asuu (Camel Pass)**, just beyond the tunnel leading to the Suusamyr valley. It's said to have the longest slope in Kyrgyzstan, though not very steep. Skiers have the choice of skiing down to the lift, or continuing on to ski down to the valley. If you continue on to the valley, you'll need to arrange with a driver to pick you up there and bring you back to the lift.

How to get to the bases without your own transport:
- Join Mihail Mihailovich on one of his trips (see above).
- Contact **Snow Land** (10 microrayon, supermarket Narodnyi; Tel: 697381). People can meet outside the snow land office and an organizer will take people to a base as long as at least eight people show up. There is usually no problem assembling the minimum group size on weekends. Round-trip transport costs about 200-250 som.
- Rent a vehicle. One firm with much experience in taking passengers to ski bases is Sergey Uriev (Tel: 670591; mobile: 580484) who has 6-17 seat minivans/minibuses available. Trips to the local ski bases – Orusai, Norus, Tugus Bulak - run a reasonable 1500-1600 som.
- Contact the slopes. Oftentimes the slopes will send a vehicle into town to pick up potential skiers. Call to find out when and where you can find these.
- Check online (diesel.kg) where people driving to ski resorts often offer rides.

The roads there can be rough, icy and uphill. If you do have your own transport, don't risk it unless you have four-wheel drive and preferably, chains.

The **Khan's Grave** is a holy site 16 kilometers (10 miles) from Bishkek, on the way to Ala-Archa (near Chonarik village, by the blue arch at the turn-off to Dzhal). It was built in honor of Kyrgyz tribal leader Baitik Batir (1820-1886) who is remembered for freeing Kyrgyzstan from Khokand rule and uniting it with Russia. Women visit the monument to pray for a mate or a child. A little futher back into the cemetery is a tall black metal structure with an Arabic rock in front. This is the grave of Batir's main assistant Boshkoi Batir Ozber-bai (1820-1911).

Next to the Khan's Grave, and on the main road to Ala-Archa, is an **ostrich farm** (look for the writing on the fence). This farm was featured in the Kyrgyz film, Birds of Paradise. From a beginning of two birds, the owner now has 34. When he reaches 50, he'll begin to distribute them within Kyrgyzstan. For 20-50 som, you can visit the ostriches. An ostrich egg goes for 3,000 som.

The **Ala-Archa** park (entrance: 30 som per person, plus additional charge for vehicles) is the closest and most easily accessible park from Bishkek. It was made into a National Park in 1985 and due to its glaciers, is the coldest canyon in the area. While the raging mountain streams, green valleys, and snow-capped peaks are captivating, the proximity to the capital (40 kilometers or 25 miles away) brings droves of visitors. You'll have to take a long hike if you really want to be alone in nature. The modern **Ala-Archa Hotel** (contact Gulida at 55-62-60 or mobile: 0502181174; Single $40, doubles $55-80, triple: $70) near the park entrance offers comfortable accommodations (7 rooms) and good views. You can get to the park by taxi (about 500 som each way), or by taking marshrutka 365 from Ahunbaeva and Manas to the end, then hitching from the park entrance to the hotel. There is a North Face store within the park grounds.

To hike to the 50 meter (164 foot)-high waterfall (takes about 2 hours):
- Take a left at the Ak-sai sign, just after the yurt on the left and across from the hotel. Stay to right at first fork. Go uphill to left, over roots, where the path continues uphill, straight and wide (and to the right of the fork, continues on a flatter course). A pretty tough uphill at beginning, followed by walk along ridge, across stream, and then up to waterfall (take left uphill at campfire site).

To visit the monument to the alpinists:
- Start at the sign (before the hotel, on the right), cross bridge, and go to left, then uphill. It's about a one hour walk).

Alemeddin (Also called *Tyoplie Kluchi*) is a beautiful ravine with several places to stay and great hiking trails. Marshrutka 373 travels there from the alamedinski bazaar, though the schedule is irregular in winter. The cheapest way to go by taxi is to take a marshrutka to Alamedinski and Ahunbaeva (called Koltso – marshrutkis 193, 269, 147 and 200 all go there). From there, you can find a taxi for 300-400 som. Hotels in the valley include:

Cois Tache (Tel: 0312 690740; café: 0312 690744), though 7 km from Tyoplie Kluchi, it has mineral water piped in. It also has a nice, large tennis court.

Closest to the canyon and the thermal pool is **Taverna 12 Kaminov (12 Chimneys)** (office at: 147a Chui Avenue, "Silk Way," 3rd floor; Tel: 0312 627761; mobile: 0503 469606; Fax: 0312 690690;

gopolicy@elcat.kg). The artfully decorated facilities include wooden cabins overlooking the river (4,000 som/night including breakfast, sleeps 4; banya 1500 som), staff in national costume and wood and stone decorations. Catering to the elite, it has a pretentious feel to it. But if you want to spend some time in the mountains and need your comforts, this might be a good option. It also has a restaurant that some make a daytrip from Bishkek to visit.

A suggested bike ride ride:

Either bike to Ala-Archa National Park (almost all uphill; go straight north on ul. Manas, turn right when can't go further, turn left onto Chondri, take a left where road curves (and another road continues straight) and continue straight to park) or take a bus there and bike back, coasting the 46 kilometers (29 miles) downhill.

TOKMOK AREA

On the way out of town from Bishkek, a roadside fruit and vegetable bazaar sells fresh fruits and veggies right from the fields in summer.

Tokmok

Pop: About 60,000

About 16 kilometers (10 miles) from Tokmok is the **Burana Tower. The 10th century tower marks the site of the Turkic Karakhanid town of Belasagun, founded in 960. This empire at one time covered an area larger than India. The ruined tower was 45 meters (147 feet), but was further damaged by Russian settlers, who used whatever bricks they could grab. In 1974 it was renovated. The museum is open from 9 until 5. A set of outdoor panels along the right of the property open up to reveal paintings and history. The tower, 6-10th century burial stones from the Western Turkic khanate (the face on each stone represents a dead hero or someone he killed) and surrounding fields and mountains are especially beautiful at sunrise and and sunset. To get there, take a taxi from Tokmok. It would also be a nice bicycle ride from Tokmok.

KARABALTA AREA

Leaving Bishkek via Karabalta, and heading south, takes you on one of the most beautiful drives in the country. After driving past fields, you'll slowly begin climbing, and continue doing so until you reach the 3,586-meter (11,765-foot) Tuya-Asuu pass, where you travel on the same plane as clouds. After traversing the 1.6 kilometer tunnel, blasted out of sheer mountain rock, you descend steeply into the broad plains of the Suusamyr valley. The road is lined with yurts selling koumiss. The first road to the left leads to Naryn. Further on, the road to Talas goes off to the right. If you continue straight, you'll cross the 3,184-meter (10,446-foot) Ala Bel Pass, then head south toward the Toktogul reservoir, a beautiful turquoise body of water, and into southern Kyrgyzstan. **If you continue on all the way to Osh, you'll experience one of the most beautiful drives in the world.

Three and a half hours south of Bishkek an attractive stone hotel and café is on the right.

Karakul

Karakul makes a good stopping over point on the way to Osh or Sary-Chelek. To get to the **Hotel Turist** when coming from the north, take a right just before the yellow and green sign on the road, then take the second right to the end of the road. The entrance is on the left. Rooms range from 380 som to $40 per person. It is a simple place, but very clean, with very hot water, and it accepts late night arrivals. It is 1.5 hours from Karakul to **Tash-Kumyr.**

Tash-Kumyr

Pop.: About 23,000

Tash-Kumyr, a long, narrow, dreary town, used to be known for coal mining, meat and tobacco plants. Now there is just a gas company there. To get to Sary-Chelek, coming from the north, take a right at the red bridge, then another right to Sary-Chelek. Tash-Kumyr is 1.5 hours from **Karakul** and four hours from **Jalalabat**. A taxi to Jalalabat costs 150 som/person.

ISSYK-KUL REGION

The magical region of Issyk-Kul is marked by Lake Issyk-Kul. It's name means "hot lake" in Kyrgyz. Despite being lined by the snow-capped Tien-Shan mountains, the lake never freezes. It is the ninth largest lake in the world by volume, and the second largest alpine lake (after Lake Titicaca). Located at 1,608 meters (5,275 feet) altitude, its depth reaches 668 meters (2,190 feet). It is 182 kilometers (113 miles) long, up to 60 kilometers (37 miles) wide and spans an area of 6,336 kilometers (2,446 square miles). The clear, serene waters and the beautiful mountain backdrop make a place that most Kyrgyz try to visit at least once, and some visit regularly. It has recently become popular with Kazakh and Russian investors and tourists. In late 2007, a Russian-Kyrgyz archeological expedition found evidence of a 2500 year old metropolis under the lake's northern shore.

The tourism centers and the best swimming beaches are centered on the northern lakeshore, especially around Cholpon-Ata. Those looking for nature, or glimpses into rural life without the commercialization will enjoy the southern shore. Karakol, located just off the eastern tip, is the administrative center for the region.

There is a 50 som fee per car traveling along Issyk-Kul if the car doesn't have Issyk-Kul region plates. A receipt is given. Higher fees (up to $20) are charged to cars from out of the country.

If driving around Issyk-Kul, be cautious of frequent cow and sheep crossings.

From the south shore of Issyk-Kul, it is easier to find transport in the mornings.

Information about the Issyk-Kul region can be found at: http://www.issyk-kul.info/, but text is currently in Russian only.

Rustam (Tel: 0502 – 522-544) is a recommended organizer of horse treks in the Issyk-Kul region.

Many of the Issyk-Kul businesses are seasonal and only operate in the summer. Three resorts open year-round are: Issyk-Kul Avrora in Bosteri, Kyrgyzskoe Vzmore in Bosteri and Rohat (Tel: (03943) 45013, 52288; Singles $26 off season, $48-84 in season; Doubles $34-69 off-season, $31-172 in season) in Kara-Oi, outside Cholpon-Ata.

Balikchy

Pop: around 40,000; phone code: 03944

Balikchy is a windy, rocky, city covered in loose plastic bags. A depressed former industrial area, there isn't much reason to stay here. Hawkers of dried fish line up near the bus stand, and near the entrance to Balikchy (between the town and the Shoestring Canyon, going toward Bishkek) the little roadside stands offer one of the best places to buy fresh fish. Just be careful to not buy fish on the endangered species list (includes *forel*).

Where to Sleep

Hotel Komfort (microregion Son-Kol, house 18, kvartira 3; Tel: 26932: This is supposed to be one of the better options in Balikchy. The apartment rooms, run by Cholpon, a local gynecologist, are rather beat up, but the sheets are fresh and clean and there is hot water for showers. Bikers are given rooms with balconies for bike storage. The biggest downer is the shared bathrooms and having to rely on the administrator to open the front door and the door to your room. The hotel is located in a quiet, residential area, with lots of children. To get there, from the Bishkek-Karakol road, turn left onto 40 let Kirgizii from the traffic circle (if coming from Bishkek). At the intersection with ul. Gagarin, follow the road that goes behind the mosque. It's one of the apartment buildings. Alternatively, take a left at the store on 144 ul. 40 let kirgizii. You can find building number 18 among the apartment buildings on the left at the top of the hill. A private room costs 150 som.

Another hotel option is **Hotel Astra**, located at ul. Chkalova 203, kv. 30. Tel: 24058.

Where to Eat

Cafe Ak-Kuu (Microrayon Son-Kul 22) is near the Comfort Hotel, in the Management Institute Building. A pleasant, clean, three-table cafe, it serves up soups (the meatball soup is good), national food, salads and blini. You can eat very well for 100 som.

Transportation

A marshrutka to **Bosteri** costs 70 som and takes about two hours.

A taxi to **Bishkek** costs 250 som/person and takes 1.5-2 hours.

Tamchy

Pop: around 1,250; phone code: 3943

Tamchy is a quiet village lined with tall, quill-like poplar trees, friendly residents, and a gorgeous lake view. The beach is pleasant and not over-touristed, a good place to enjoy the waters in solitude.

Where to Sleep

Walk down any street in town and you'll see plenty of *сдаю комнаты* (rooms for rent) signs. Prices start at a few hundred som, but owners seem willing to negotiate, especially if you visit off-season. Despite the bed-bugs and simple accommodations, I enjoyed my stay at ulitsa Zhunshalieva 12 (Tel: 21-2-73) in a room with a lakefront view. As in many other homestays, meals were available.

Sonya Sarakan (ul. Bayamanova 40; Tel: 21163) can accommodate up to 10 visitors in her giant, spotless house with garden. A light, airy, comfortable home, less than five minutes walk from the beach, it's a pleasant place to stay and an especially good choice for groups. To get there from the main road (coming from Bishkek), take a left on Chingishbaev, then take a right onto Bayamanova. It's on the left.

CBT (see Other Services below) offers several choices of homestay families in Tamchy. Lodging and breakfast costs 450 som per person; meals are 180 som each.

Altynai Osoemov (24 ul. Chyngyshbaeva; Tel: 2-11-12) accepts guest in her ethnographically designed house. It's located across from the castle and just steps from the beach.

Stari Zamok (or Old Castle) Hotel is located near the beach and the rooms are decorated in various styles – Chinese, English, French and Old Castle. Tel: 42363; 0502 615568, 0502 257462.

Where to Eat

Many homestays offer meals to order. There is also at least one café in town and a store on Manas Street.

What to Do

On the beach, you can find chairs and umbrellas available for hire at 15 som/hour each and pedal boats for 50-80 som/hour.

Transportation

A local driver, R. Kasumbekov (Tel: 5-11-53) offers one-way taxi service to **Bishkek** in an Audi for 1400 som.

You can hitch a ride with passing cars or minibuses by standing on the main street, Manas. If going to **Bishkek**, it might be faster to get a ride to **Balikchy**, then take a bus to Bishkek. The trip to Bishkek takes three hours and costs 150 som. In a full-size public bus, it takes over five hours and costs 110 som.

Other Services

The **Community Based Tourism Office** (Tel: 21272; 0773 355611; reservation@cbtkyrgyzstan.kg, cbttours@mail.ru, a_rajiev@ yahoo.com) is located at 47 Manas.

Chok-Tal

Pansionat Bityaz (Витязь) (Tel: (0343) 43326; 0502-872719; Fax: 03943-23207) is located on a nice stretch of beach west of Cholpon Ata. It's on the cheaper end of sanatoriums, but remains popular with Kazakhs and can fill up in summer. $15/person for standard room, $25 for pol-luks, $35 for luks, including meals.

Other options in the area include: **Kooperator** (Tel: (03943) 21384; 0517 738042; 130 beds); **Progress** (Tel: 0502 664774, 45 beds); **Lazurni Bereg** (Tel: (03943) 42666, (0312) 580011, 23215, 23216); **Nasip y Nur**, 300 beds and **Royal Beach** (Tel: (03943) 42777, 42778; (0502) 358375, 23176, 23289; 130 beds).

Cholpon-Ata

Phone code: 3943

Cholpon-Ata is Issyk-Kul tourist-central, the congregation point for visitors to the summer resorts. This is the place to find any services you might need – banks, internet, cafes, post office, groceries, lots of lodging options. If you want to experience local life or have a less crowded beach experience, other options around the lake are better.

Where to Sleep

In town you'll find the **Sunrise mini pension** (ul. Kalinina 26; Tel: (03943) 45115, (0312) 547302, 658765).

Additional options in Cholpon-Ata include:

Monts (Tel: (03943) 35512, 44164; 0502 322016).

Ala-Too (Tel: (03943) 43973, 43560). Works year round.

Bereke (03943) 43797.

Ak-Chardak (03943) 43433, 20370; (0312) 584285.

Ak Tilek (03943) 42217, 42598

Where to Eat

Recommended cafes that are open year-round include: **Café Versal**, **Café Rybak** and **Café Green Pub**. In the summer, outdoor cafes proliferate.

For a very cheap meal, look behind the covered bazaar on the right just as you are leaving the city towards Bosteri. There you can find *lagman* and other local dishes served on long tables.

What to Do

The highlight of a visit to Cholpon-Ata and to Issyk-Kul are the **petroglyphs. Only two kilometers north off the main road, it's worth trying to stop by here enroute to other places on the lake. An entire field of glacial boulders display engravings of deer, wolves, hunters and ibex. They date from 500 BC to 100 AD and are thought to have been created by the Usun and Sak peoples. Admission is 25 som, collected by a warden who lives near the rocks.

The recently rebuilt **Kashkul-Ata museum** sits on a stunning lakeshore location. Against the backdrop of dark blue waters and vast, manicured lawns, it showcases monuments to famous Kyrgyz poets,

Manas legends, theatre and Orthodox, Muslim, Buddhist and Jewish faiths. It was built by Kyrgyz political deputy and Balikchy native T.J. Kereksizov and later sold to investors. Tickets cost 200 som for Kyrgyz citizens, 300 som for foreigners.

The **regional museum** (ul. Sovietskaya 69) is closed on Sundays.

The **M. Avesov House-museum-library** can be found with the marker to the left near the entrance to the city from the north.

You can rent a boat or look into cruises at the **Kruiz Yacht Club** (ul. Akmatbai-Ata 25; Tel: (03943) 42883, 43373).

Transportation

A marshrutka to **Karakol** costs 100 som and takes about two hours.

A marshrutka to **Bishkek** costs 250 som and takes 180 minutes. A taxi costs 400 som/person and takes 150 minutes. Expect a 30-50% increase in prices in summer.

You can call a taxi by dialing 177. A shared taxi to the **Dead Lake** costs 800 som per person (4 places).

Other Services

ATF Bank and **Halyk Bank** have ATM machines. All local banks change dollars and euros.

Bosteri

Phone code: 3943

A smaller, cozier place than Cholpon-Ata, Bosteri is used to the tourists and offers most of the products and services visitors might want. Several sanatoria line the Bosteri beach area, including one of the most popular, *Kyrgyzoe Bzmore*.

Where to Sleep

In high season, call ahead, as some places fill up for several weeks solid. Private houses for rent post signs (сдаю ком-ты) all along the northern shore road. Sometimes, women stand at the intersections, advertising apartments for rent, ready to bring you to their spare apartment. Take a look at a private home or apartment before accepting, but these options are generally safe and a good way to put some of the income from tourism into local's pockets.

Operating year-round, the giant **Kyrgyzskoe Vzmore (Tel: (03943) 35549, 43210; Kyrgyz_seaside@ktnet.kg) remains one of the most popular sanatorium among locals. Most of the 1000 spaces offer lake views. Prices include three meals a day in the common dining room as well as treatments including an indoor swimming pool filled with heated lake water, mineral water baths, mud scrubs, aromatherary, and the unique underground salt caves, said to cure respiratory problems. Prices are about 20% cheaper without treatment. Prices per person range from 740 to 7000 in April and October-December; 820-8100 in May, 900-9300 in June and September, and 1000-11500 in July and August. Four-person cottages cost $150-600. The complex's beach is large and well-maintained. The atmosphere is an intriguing mix of Soviet sanatoria with seaside relaxation. If alone, it's easy to meet others in the dining hall. Meals are plentiful, but stock up on snacks and drinks in town to avoid the inflated resort prices.

Constructed in 2001, **Talisman Village** (Tel: 36527, 36528, (0312) 650019; Fax: (0312) 650380; www.talisman.in.kg; tvillage@mail. kg) is an upscale resort oriented to families, professionals and people seeking a quiet rest. Rooms are built into cottages and townhouses and include TV, refrigerator and modern bathroom. The beds are unfortunately hard and flies can be a problem in summer. The quality of food is among the best of Issyk-Kul resorts and the beach is quiet and relaxing in the day, too dark at night. Room rates (for a double room, including three meals a day for both occupants, range from $50 (December to April) to $100 in August.

During Soviet times, each government institution had its own resort for its employees. **Pansionat Tulpar** (Tel: (03943) 35567 or 36354) is the resort belonging to the Kyrgyz Prom-Stroi bank. Bank employees still rest here at discounted rates, but it is also open to others. It's a mid-level resort, with clean, comfortable rooms, friendly service and decent food, but a step down from the Kyrgyzskoe Vosmore. It is the closest resort to Bosteri town. The market, shops and internet café are only a ten-minute walk away. Rooms include refrigerator and TV, but hot water is available only two times a day. In summer, a first-floor room facing away from the lake would be the coolest and quietest option. Prices, per person, including three meals a day are: January to mid-June 300-1200, mid-June to July 1 1000-2100, July 2 through August 1400-2300, August 31 to September 2 1000-2100, September 2 through December 300-1200.

In high season, group tours are available daily to the nearby canyons, Jeti-Oguz and the dead lake for 200-600 som/person.

Issyk-Kul Avrora (Tel: (03943) 37215 43543, 95345, 37348; 0502 529407; Fax: 37211; Bishkek Tel/Fax: (0312) 662571; singles 1600-1800 som out of season, 2700-3000 in season; doubles 3200-6600 out of season; 2700-5600 in season) is an Issyk-Kul landmark, a giant complex that was the destination for Soviet dignitaries. It remains a central point in the summer beach scene.

The owners of **Umut internet café** (Tel: 36220) rent out 2-room apartments for 1000 som/day.

The **Golden Sands (Zolotie Peski) Pansionat**, known for its discos and beach-front attractions, is popular with youth looking for action and entertainment. In summers, its beach is packed.

Where to Eat

If staying at a sanatorium, stock up on snacks and drinks in the village, where they will be much cheaper than the overpriced items in the isolated sanatoria. Vendors at the main intersection sell fresh fruits and vegetables.

What to Do

**The Sunday market (held on Saturdays and Sundays in summer, Sundays in winter) is reason enough to spend a Saturday evening in Bosteri. The market starts up by 7 and continues on until four. Full of local color, products and motion, it's an Issyk-Kul highlight.

Transportation

Taxis travel from the village's central intersection to the sanatoria along the shore. Buses and taxis frequently travel between Cholpon-Ata and Bosteri, as well as along the Issyk-Kul road. Taxis and *marshrutkis* congregate at the central intersection.

Other Services

Internet is available for a steep 60 som/hour at **Café Umut** (near the intersection by the bazaar; Tel: 36220)

The **revolving staircase**, on the right when coming from the north, just after the long, fenced compound of the President's house is worth a stop for a beautiful view of mountains on one side and the lake on the other. Off season, it doesn't revolve, but entrance is free. Excellent view.

Komsomol

The first village after Bosteri, you can find apartments for rent by calling 0502-718205.

Karagai-Bulak

In this village, just before Grigorevka when coming from Cholpon-Ata, look for the ancient grave near a soccer field by a bus stand. It's visible from the road.

Grigorevka

Shortly before Grigorevka, when coming from Cholpon-Ata, is a marked turn off to **Chong Ak-Suu Canyon, also called *Grigorevskoe ushele*. A pristine river runs along the base of a steep, forested canyon. Hire a driver (can be found through hotels or at taxi stands in most lakeshore towns) to take you through the canyon. There is a small lake at the end. It's a rough ride, but an amazing view. Or just go partway in for a picnic, camping, or overnight at a small hotel. Some hotels run group day trips here.

Semyonovka

In the small, friendly village of Semyonovka, you can find the turn-off to the **Kichi Ak-Suu canyon,** also called *Semenovskoye ushele*. In comparison with the green beauty and water of Grigorevskoe, Semenovskoye is a more open space, filled with grasses and flowers. Horses are available for rent to visit a lake. Hire a driver to take you there (available at hotels or at taxi stands in most lakeshore towns) or look into daytrips offered by hotels. This is a good area for camping.

Across the Kozhayar river is the impressive marble monument to Sadir-Ake (1821-1905). It was built by Rysbek Akmatbayev, an Issyk-Kul native who became a political deputy and leader in the criminal world. He was murdered in 2006.

Ananyevo

Pop: about 12,000; phone code: 03942

Ananyevo is a former Cossack settlement with a Russian population that remains higher than usual. It's named after captain Nikolai Ananyev, who died, together with 700 soldiers from the area – almost its entire male population – on the western front of the Soviet Union during World War II. A quiet, off-the-beaten track spot, it's a place to spend a little time on the lake without the tourists.

Where to Sleep

Lesic, a Swiss development organization, operates the two guesthouses in town. The nicer house (ul. Almatinskaya 76; Tel: 61455) is run by a friendly administrator, Natasha. Included in the $10/night charge is breakfast and a fantastic banya. Lunch and dinner are available for $3 each. A common room has a TV, videos and stereo and the kitchen is packed with pots and dishes for cooking. Lesic also has a smaller, simpler house available. To get there:

-From Tyup: take a right on ulitsa Almatinskaya. Go straight toward the mountains. At the 3-way fork, continue straight. It's on the right.

-From main intersection, take the road up toward the mountains. Notice mural and statue on right. Take first road to right after that. It's at the second crossroad, on the right. Green house.

Where to Eat

There is a pelmeni café on the left on the way to the lake, another small café nearby, and an outdoor summer café, as well as several sizeable shops.

What to Do

To get to the lake, walk towards the water from the main intersection. Go straight for 3 kilometers. Look at view at first beach, but continue on for swimming areas.

There is a great mural on a building on the right as you head toward the mountains from the main intersection.

Transportation

Ananyevo is 50 kilometers (31 miles) from Cholpon Ata and 90 kilometers (56 miles) from Karakol. It is well connected by marshrutkis and taxis that run around the lakeshore. In Ananyevo, you can find the taxis and marshrutkis congregated at the central intersection.

Kuturgu

This is the only place between Tyup and Ananyevo where you can find a meal. The village includes a café, stolovaya, and nearer the lake, a restaurant and lodging at the Pansionat Drujba (Tel: (0312) 58-2066).

Additional lodging options in northern Issyk-Kul

If you arrive in high season without reservations, you may need to call around to find a place with vacancies. Additional lodging options along the north shore of Lake Issyk-Kul include:

Intimak (Tyup region)

Fakel (03945) 37423.

Karagai-Bulak

Pensionat Cinegore, Tel: (03943) 42552; 42877; (0312) 585816.
Pensionat Belek, Tel: (03943) 35758.

Korumdu

Neptune, Tel: (03943) 37075, 37281; (0312) 665499, 663401; (0502) 573818, 545592.
Resthouse Aalam, Tel: 35804.
Pansionat Tulpar, Tel: (03943) 35567; 35198.
Issyk-Kul, Tel: 3-56-96; mobile: 344986.
Murok, Tel: 35709, 35896.
Sayakat (03943) 30503.

Solemar (03943) 30438; (0502) 578883.
Sinegore (03943) 42877, 42552.
Ohotni Dvor (03943) 30542, 42237; (0502) 735636.
Chon Ak-Suu (03943) 64524.
Dalni Kordon (0502) 328751.
Kirchin (0517) 738510.
Akdanis hotel club (ul. Druzhba 8; (0502) 530326; (0502) 823737

Bulan-Sogotu

Zhashtyk (03943) 37225, 52150.

Bosteri

U Saida – hotel, sauna, massage in Bosteri itself (03943) 35292.
Kazakhstan Sanatorium (03943) 42220, 42000, 43528; Fax: (03943)
42269.
Salamat (03943) 44424.
Defin de Luks (0502) 571350.
Marmelad Village Rest Area (0502) 323000.
Gulkayir (03943) 35787, 35353, 715203.
Orbita (03943) 35105, 44121.
Tolkun (03943) 35347, 35477; (0312) 483202.
Alma-Ati (03943) 45142, 45143, 35733; Fax: (03272) 553103;
almaata@glotur.kz)
Issyk-Kul (03943) 35696, 35604; (0502) 344986.
Ilbirs (03943) 35679.
Ilbirs Saadat (0502 321514.
Bonur (03943) 35055.
Delfin (03943) 35457, 425565.
Altyn Tor (0502) 572646; (03943) 35694.
Luchezarnoe Poberezhe (03943) 42277, 36017; (0502) 266739.
Turan Azia (03943) 35476, 35257; (0502) 571418.
Keremet (03943) 35257; (0502) 571278.
Dostuk (03943) 35238, 45159.
Murok (03943) 35709; (0502) 400252.
Asyl Tash (03943) 42756.
Saamal (03943) 35348.
Aalam (03943) 35808; (0502) 233447.
Belek (03943) 35758.
Flamingo (03943) 37501, 52886.

Kara-Oi

Rahat: (03943) 54419
Ak-Bermet (03943) 42919, 54071; akbermet@mail.ru
Smeraldo Bich (0517) 788087, 23176.
Altyn-Kol (03943) 45034, 52403, 42147, 45134. Works year round.
Dan Em Servis (0502) 492002. Operates all year.
Azat (03943) 21270; 0502 331315.
Kara-Oi (03943) 54087, 45015; 0502 220321.
Beli Parohod (03943) 42482, 52168; 0502 572743.
Komvolshik (03943) 45061, 0502 387879.
Dilorom (03943) 45038. Works year round.
Ak-Bermet (03943) 43219, 54071, 45010, 42789; Fax: (03943)
42919. Open all year.
Akun Issyk-Kul (0502 124362; (03943) 43683, 42072, 43504,
52133. Works year round.
Kunostu Zhek (03943) 42405; 0502 517672.

Chon-Sari-Oi

Altyn Kum (03943) 42924; 65129; 0502 787271. Operates year-round.
Yamaika (03943) 57529; 0502 320831; hotel_jamaica@mail.ru.
Operates year-round.
**Raduga (Tel: (03943) 57555; 0502 517682; 0502 511504) is
one of the most modern and comfortable hotels on the Issyk-Kul
shores. The 62 double rooms are newly built with private bathrooms,
televisions and refrigerators.
Zolotoi Rodnik (0502) 270902, 57609.
Geolog (03943) 52965; (0502) 898053, 45130.
Deniz (03943) 57640, 324525.
Asyl (03943) 57581, 57505.
Agroorganik Chaika (03943) 57518, 57576. Open year-round.
Ak-Maral (0502) 325408, 42212.
Aist (0502) 292894, 45148.

Kara Choi Oy

Meder Pensionat (0517) 716503, 0502 344589, (03943) 56357
Lazurni Bereg pensionat (03943) 42666; 0502 328101

Kosh-Kol

(just before Tamchy when coming from Balikchy):
Kyrgyz Tani Pansionat: (03943) 21304, 0502 647859. 175 beds.
Operates in summer.
Ak-Zhol Pansionat (03943) 21191; 0502 344775. 300 beds.
Operates year-round.
Zolotoi Trebas Pansionat (03943) 21397; 0502 326753. 100 beds,
open summer only.
Kelecheck (Tel: 0502 376583; 21308). 200 beds, open summer only.
Pansionat Zhildiz (Tel: 2-12-31, 2-1271, 2-12-62; 0503 27-21-36).
240 beds, open in summer.
Golubaya Buhta Pansionat (03943) 21293, 21142. 170 beds,
operates in summer.
Dordoi Pansionat (Tel: 0517 781685; 792183; Fax: (0312) 690044).
55 beds, open in summer.
Ecolog Plus Pansionat (03943) 21107; 0502 545235. 48 beds, open
in summer.

Toru-Aigyr

Mayak Resort: (3944) 24305, (0502) 289184, 295423, 268458.
Located on a bay, it appears to be a nice place for kids. There isn't
much nearby besides Oasis Sport Fishing, Tel: (3944) 24305.

TYUP REGION

Tyup

Pop: about 13,500; phone code: 03945

Tyup is a quiet, attractive, largely untouristed village. The agricultural town can seem to house more cows than people. Large mountains rise up nearby, offering a view that resembles an oil painting. It's a good place for a glimpse of village life or as a stop on the road to the Karkara Valley. It's also a convenient place to venture out to the Burial Mounds of Sak tribe Scythian warriors and nobles and the historical hamlet of Svetly Mys, where many buildings survive from a 19th century Russian Orthodox monastery. Just outside Tyup, on the way to Karakol, is a canal that serves as a popular summer swimming hole for locals. Watch swimmers bob happily amidst views of expansive green fields and a covering blue sky while cows graze nearby.

Where to Sleep

Shaidylda and his wife Anarkul run a cozy, friendly **guesthouse in their home (ul. Belinski 1; Tel: 21411; scheidylda@rambler.ru). It belongs to the CBT network. Lodging with breakfast costs 400 som per night per person; meals run 250 som each. Shaidelda offers guide services throughout Kyrgyzstan and his wife and daughter make and sell high-quality souvenirs. Call before arriving and they'll meet you in the center of Tyup to guide you to their home. Shaidylda is fluent in German and speaks a little English.

AK-SUU REGION

Karakol

Pop: Around 65,000; phone code: 03922

Karakol is a jewel of an attraction year round, offering the best skiing in Kyrgyzstan in the winter, and a variety of mountain activities in the summer. Visitors can find the full range of accommodations and services – from budget to comfort. The small wooden houses give the town an air of the Russian past, as does the wooden church and the nearby museum and monument to the famous Russian explorer Nikolai Przhevalsky.

Karakol was founded by Russian settlers in the 19th century and grew when explorers came to map the mountains separating Kyrgyzstan from China. In the 1880s, many Dungans, Chinese Muslims, flowed into the town, fleeing persecution in China. Nikolai Przhevalsky died of typhoid in Karakol in 1888, while preparing for an expedition to Tibet. The town was renamed Przhevalsk after him. Local protest returned the name of Karakol in 1921, but that decision was reversed in 1939. It remained Przhevalsk until the end of the Soviet Union in 1991.

Coming into Karakol from the southern shore, you'll arrive on ulitsa Tokotgul. Continue straight to the city center. To continue around to the north shore, take the 2nd left after passing TSUM, the central department store, then stay to the right at the fork four kilometers out of town.

Where to Sleep

For simple but comfortable, central accommodation, try the new **Hotel Issyk-Ata** (ul. Alibakova 145; Tel: 20848; When looking at the central square from TSUM, it's on the street to the left of the square, directly across the street from the park, on the 2nd floor). The hotel has 14 places in clean rooms for 200-300 som/night/person. A nice single includes a TV and a private bath. The hotel is open 24 hours, has hot water and is conveniently located right next door to an internet club.

Turkestan Yurt Camp (ul. Toktogula 273; Tel: 29582; 59896; 26489; psi@karakol.kg; http://www.karakol.kg/en/; in Bishkek, tel: 511560 or mobile (0543) 911451); when facing Tsum, walk to the right along Toktogul. It's on the left, a few minutes from the central area). One of the most centrally located budget options, it offers lodging in yurts, tents and rooms. The rooms, which cost 10-15 euro in summer, are discounted to 300 som/night (without breakfast) in winter – a good value. Yurt accommodation is 6 euro with shower, 4 without sheets or shower; or 30 euro for an entire yurt. Breakfast costs 3 euro and lunch/dinner 4 euro. Also offers laundry, internet and baggage storage.

Gulnara's Guesthouse (67 ul. Stahanova; Tel: (03922) 55544) has four cozy rooms in a comfortable, neat home for 350-400 som/night, including breakfast. Dinner is available for 100-120 som; laundry for 40 som/kilo, internet one som/minute. It is one of the better value options in the city. To walk there from the city center, take ul. Toktogula across the river, take a left on Kravtsova, take a right on Stahanova at the shop U Irin and continue to 67.

Greenyard Guesthouse (ul. Novostroyka 14; Tel (03922) 29801; mobile: (0502) 56 04 67; green-yard@rambler.ru) is the most European of the local guesthouses and is popular with international consultants. It's pricy by local standards, located on the very edge of the city (on the border with a neighboring village), cold in the winter and not as hospitable as other places. Rooms with breakfast cost 700 som, a place in the yurt including three meals is 650-800 som. Other services include laundry (50-100 som, lunch 150 som, dinner 150-250 som, guide-porter $15/day, horse riding 70-350 som, interpreter 500-800 som per day/ transport 10 som/km, and falcon hunting $50. Better service can be found for better value.

Other options include:

Valentina B&B (Pionerskaya 3; Tel: 41583; 350 soms/person).

Guest House Teskey (Asanalieva 44, near Oktyabrskaya street; Tel: 26268; 400 som/person).

Jamilya's B&B (34b ul. Shopokova; Tel: 43019; 500 som/person)

Galas Group of Apartment and B&B (Tel: 51155, Galina; 250-350 som/person)

Guest House "Elita" (ul. Kutmanalieva 56; Tel: 50150; 450, 650 and 850 som/person)

Hotel Issyk-Kul (ul. Fuchina 38). For the state-owned part, contact Kalmira at 29673. For the privately owned section, contact Kyial at 59000.

Amir Guest House (ul. Amanbaev 78; Tel: 51315; $39 single, $56 double, including breakfast).

For a modern, comfortable stay in the mountains, try the **Gorno Lizhnaya Ideal Tur Turbaza** (Tel: 531870 or 582428 in Bishkek; (3922) 51454 or 51494 in Karakol; pmz@exnet.kg). During high season, book at least a week or two in advance. Prices are $50 for rooms, $200 for an 8-10 person cottage. Meals are available for 15 euros/day. Even with a reservation, you could find yourself without a room if a political deputy comes to visit. In winter, you'll need a strong car or chains to make it up the mountain.

Where to Eat

**Café Fakir (ul, Gorkovo, near intersection with Toktogula; across the street from Tsum) has undoubtedly the best food in Karakol, and a wide enough selection to allow you to eat there several times a day without getting tired of the food. The selection includes large and fresh salads (25-50), Chinese, fish, meat, soups, local dishes, and desserts, including blini with ice cream and chocolate and fruit or chocolate cocktails. English menu available.

**Café Zarima (ul. Toktogula) offers a nice selection of salads, soups, local and European dishes at slightly lower prices than Fakir. Unfortunately, some of the best options need to be ordered in advance. Good service and good value.

Kench (ul. Telmen, near the statue, located kiddy korner from the red-topped poles) is a European-style café, with a pleasant interior and mediocre food. Along with Fakir and Kalinka, a favorite among foreigners.

Kalinka (intersection of Koinko and Abdurakmanova; Open 10-10 Monday-Saturday) has a troop of sullen wait staff who serves up rather bland Russian food (including *blini* and *vareniki*) within a pretty, carved wooden interior. Closed Sundays.

Ashkana Blinnaya (1 ul. Torgoeva, near intersection with Toktogul, across from stadium; Open daily 8-8) is a clean, pleasant, bright one-room café, with nothing on the menu over 28 som. A good place for a snack, especially for *blini* or milk products (try the *tvorog* with cream and sugar).

Café Uyut (Уют) (green building near market) is packed with locals at lunchtime. It serves primarily national food – *manti, lagman, borsh* – with almost everything on the menu under 40 som. There is no toilet on the premises.

What to Do

The **Przhevalsky Museum is one of the highlights of Karakol. Located seven kilometers (4.3 miles) outside of town, it is a pleasant excursion into the countryside and offers a view of Lake Issyk-Kul. If you speak Russian or bring a translator, the guided tour included in the 50 som admission is well-worth listening to. There are also some English translations on the exhibits. Built in 1957, the museum currently attracts 2,000 foreign visitors a year. The attractive 10 hectare (25 acre) park grounds contain a monument to Przhevalsky, his grave, and a monument to Karasai Ulu Kuseiin. To enter the grounds, push hard on the right gate. The museum is open daily, year round, from 9-4, within a break from 1-2. Try to arrive a while before closing time, as the keepers seem to disappear if there are no visitors. To get there you can take a taxi, take a bus marked *dachi* (on Lomanosova street, across from the Bugu market; 10 som, look for museum sign on the right), or bike in the summer.

The **Gorno Lizhnaya Ideal Tur Turbaza (Tel: 531870 or 582428 in Bishkek; ul. Tynistanova 17; Tel: (3922) 51454 or 51494 in Karakol; http://www.karakol-ski.com) is located about 12 kilometers (7.5 miles) from town and offers ski rental and downhill skiing from January on. This is the best skiing in Kyrgyzstan and is a must-visit in the winter. The base is at 2300 meters (7,545 feet) and the trails go up to 3040 meters (9,973 feet). A hotel and café constructed in 2005 (see above) make it a modern and pleasant ski base. Vegetarian meals are available. A ticket for the 5 lifts costs 250 som/day (150 children), 50 som for the sled lift. Ski rental is 400 som, snowboards 500, sleds 50. Lessons with an instructor costs 500 som/day or 200/hour. There are also snowmobile rides available. To get there:

- Take a car with strong wheels and chains (it's uphill and slick)
- Take a taxi to the nearest village (about 100 som) and walk about an hour
- Take marshrutka 101 to Kashka-suu park entrance (5 som) and walk about 1.5 hours
- Head up with the ski base workers by meeting the vehicle at the Comet sign (ul. Pervomaiskaya and Alibakova) at 7 a.m., returning at 5 p.m.) – 50 som.

On the way to the base, you will pass through Karakol National Park and will have to pay the admission fee.

The Places of Kyrgyzstan – Karakol

The ski base employees headed up the mountain in a giant green, military-like vehicle (called a *vahovka*). They were going up to work at the Karakol ski base, one of the most modern and popular in Kyrgyzstan. Almost 20 people, mostly men, squeezed along the three benches. Though it was early and still dark, they were in good humor from the previous day's holiday, Men's Day (called Defenders of the Motherland Day in Soviet times). One man passed chocolates around.

"I was up late and my head hurts," the friendly man who handles ski rentals told me. "There was vodka and beer and a sauna and girls."

They seemed like a nice team. Seeing the grey, worn look to the people in Karakol, and hearing of the poverty and low wages there, I was glad to see so many individuals heading to stable jobs.

On the way to Karakol, I had seen so much new development taking place along the shores of Issyk-Kul, people hurrying to finish hotels and business premises before the summer season opened. Many of the structures were new, bright, and almost gauche, especially when one was placed directly next to a small, decaying wooden house. I worried that the rich and the criminals were taking over all the good areas and business opportunities.

But seeing this base at Karakol reminded me that expensive ventures also create jobs. Granted, virtually no one from Karakol could afford even a day's ski rental and lift ticket, much less a night's stay at the mountain hotel. However, the new ski facilities, the increase in tourism, and the higher demand for lodging and food provided stable jobs for the poorer of the area. Though the rich continued to get richer, the poor began to do a little better.

After getting my skis, I headed toward the slopes, first stopping at the picnic tables where locals gathered to sled and eat. From that vantage point, I could see the skiers lining up for the chairlift. They were dressed in blues, purples, yellows, greens and reds, like so many jelly beans. A well-built man skied down the slope in nothing but a little pair of blue shorts, his brown body shimmering under the mountain sun. Another man skied without poles, holding a baby in his arms as he went up the chairlift. He skied back down with the baby facing forward, smiling.

In comparison, the locals wore only black and dark blue. They carried bags of onions, huge thermoses of tea, plastic bags full of round white bread, and satchels of food for their picnic lunches. A group of men surrounded the skis I'd taken off, prodding the material, putting their feet in the attachments. Only one man among them had skis, which he used to walk up a small hill, then ski down, unable to afford a lift ticket. His narrow, weak, wooden skis looked like someone had carved them by hand. He asked me to trade. I wished I could. Although at least where we stood and talked, there was no admission fee. The rich had their privileges, but the locals could still feel the warm mountain sun alight their faces and smell the pine and ice crystals.

Wonderful snow, fresh mountain air, spectacular views of forested peaks and foggy valleys that changed with each trip up the chair lift characterized the skiing at Karakol. The only disappointing aspect was the chairlifts – t-bars and individual poles that require standing and often inspire falling. But even these had their good points. Paired with random people on the t-bar, listening to the clank of the cable, I was able to enter conversations with a variety of characters.

As the metal bar pressed our bottoms upward, I met an investor and director of a major bottled drink manufacturer. I rode up with the nephew of a government deputy, who bragged to me how their family showed up with no reservations, but the fully-booked hotel cleared out two rooms for them. A local teacher of tourism told me the base allowed him and his students to ski in return for helping out around the facilities. One woman came all the way from Omsk, in Siberia. I met a man from Bishkek who wanted to go home on Saturday so he'd have time to plant apple trees in his yard on Sunday.

Vitaly, a young ethnic Russian businessman from Bishkek, told me that two years earlier, he'd owned two small electronics shops. He took a bank loan for $20,000.

"I imported my goods from the United Arab Emirates," he said. "As soon as I took that loan, I suddenly became a wholesaler, rather than a retail buyer. I got big discounts on my purchases and everything changed. Overnight, I reached a place that it would have taken me two to three years to reach." He smiled at the memory.

He now has five shops and a $100,000 credit line.

With fresh powder snow, no lines, and few people, I often felt like I had the entire mountain to myself. After lunch, some paragliders flew off the top of the mountain. They wore skis and bent their legs as though they were skiing on air. They floated over the pine trees, over the mountain tops, looking out at Lake Issyk-Kul.

"Whoo-hee!" one of them cried out, as he rose up into the air, higher than the two falcons that live at the mountaintop.

Take a hike in **Karakol National Park**. The entrance is five kilometers from town and the Karakol and Kashka-Suu Canyons offer good hiking and sledding possibilities.

The wooden **Dungan mosque** was created by Chinese artisans between 1907 and 1910 and built without a single metal nail. It is made from blue-grey brick with a wooden cupola instead of a minaret.

The wooden **Russian Orthodox church**, called the Holy Trinity Cathedral, was completed in 1895, replacing a stone church that was destroyed in an earthquake. The Soviets used it as a club but it was restored in the early 1990s and is now being used again.

If you can pull yourself out of bed early in the morning, you won't regret a trip to the **lifestock market**. Walk amidst cows, horses and sheep and watch locals from all over the area as they purview and compare them. The bustle and activity is all the more impressive under the ridge of mountains on the horizon and the emerging sun. Dress warmly in winter and be careful of sudden streams. Go as early as you can. The activity is over by 10 a.m.

The nearby hot **mineral springs** at Altyn-Arashan and Jety-Oguz and the **alpine lake** of Ala-Kol are popular trekking destinations.

Transportation

Karakol is a very walkable city, with even the most distant places no more than a half hour or so from the center. Many of the roads are dirt and a walk is a nice way to take in the local architecture, livestock, and street life.

Taxis from Bishkek leave from the zapadni (western) station and cost 450-500 som per passenger and take about 5 hours. Marshrutkis cost 250 som and take six hours.

A marshrutka to Cholpon-Ata costs 90 som and takes about two hours.

Taxis can easily be found in the city center or ordered through taxi services (including City Taxi Tel: 161 or 0502 51-06-06 – the driver gives you a coupon after each ride. Collect nine coupons and the 10th ride is free – and Salam Taxi – 22222). Marshrutkis and buses also run regularly, both within Karakol and to surrounding communities.

Marshrutkis and taxis go from the bus station to town. It's about a 20 minute walk from the center on LenCom (Akunalayeva) and Prezhevalski. From the center, walk down Toktogul past Turkestan camp (on your left). Take a left at the first stoplight. A gas station is on the corner. Walk 10-15 minutes to Przhevalski, the first intersection (stoplight) past the mosque. You can see the cars and buses. From the station, take marshrutka 111 to the market.

To get to the beach, head 4 kilometers out of town, toward the north shore. At the fork, take a left (or hitch a ride) to the beach.

Other Services

You can change dollars for som at Krygyzstan Commerical Bank (AKB) (ul. Toktogul and Gebze, near Tsum) or at ATF Bank (almost across the street from AKB, next to the gas station). AKB also changes travelers checks. Euros can be difficult to change.

The **Tourist Information Center** (Tel: 23425; info@issyk-kul-info.kg) is located at 130 ulitsa Abdrakhmanova.

The **Community Based Tourism Office** is located at 123 ulitsa Abdrahmanov (Tel: 55000; 0772 203087; cbtkarakol@rambler.ru), across the street from the Tourist Information Center.

For excellent **guide services**, contact Valery Serebrennikov (23 ul. Gorkovo; Tel: 26939; cell: (0543) 940347; boroda46@rambler.ru) or Ainura Adylbekova (ul. Sovietskaya 23/2; Tel: (0543) 918378; Leventik1@yandex.ru or ainura.adylbekova.uca@gmail.com). They train tourism students at the university and are passionate, knowledgeable and friendly people, dedicated to the outdoors. They both speak some English, Ainura's is quite good. They can organize few-day hikes to Jeti-Oguz, to alpine Lake Ala-Kol and to the Altyn-Arashan hot mineral springs, as well as more adventurous treks, including winter free-style skiing.

Turkestan (ul. Toktogula 273; Tel: 59896, 26489; Fax: 59896; turkestan@karakol.kg; http://www.karakol.kg/en/about_en/) is a local tour agency that also runs the Turkestan Yurt Camp (above). They offer trekking, climbing, cultural and horseback trips, as well as helicopter flights over the Tien-Shan.

Most necessities can be found at **Tsum**, where a banner hangs in front, reading "President --- (formerly Akaev) guarantees stability and wellbeing." Several shops around the area stock a wide range of products. There is no need to stock up on supplies in Bishkek.

Internet is available at ul. Alibakova 145. When looking at the central square from TSUM, it's on the street to the left of the square, directly across the street from the park, on the 2nd floor. Another option is Café Molodozh, on ulitsa Toktogula 263, #42.

Karakol Bikes (Tel: 26939; karakolbikes@gmail.com) is the first local organization to offer mountain bike trips in the Issyk-Kul region. Revenues are used to support the students in the guide school mountain tourism program. New Giant bikes with front suspension, grip shifters and V-brakes are available, as are helmets.

Ak-Suu

Ak-Suu is best known for its hot mineral spring baths that are said to cure everything from rheumatism to insomnia. You can visit for a bath (25 som) or stay in the sanatorium for about 130 som/night, including simple meals. Ak-Suu is easily reached by marshrutka from Karakol, seven kilometers away.

Jeti-Oguz

Phone code: 03946

Jeti-Oguz village is set three kilometers off the main road. It boasts an interesting World War II statue. The canyon, famous red rocks, and sanatorium are another 14 kilometers (8.7 miles) uphill. The canyon is 2200 meters (7,218 feet) above sea level. The reserve, which covers 31,800 hectares (78,579 acres), is located in the Jeti-Oguz river basin, on the Teskey Ala-Too slopes. Established in 1958 and filled with mountain streams, pine hills and pastures, the area offers great hiking, camping and picknicking opportunities. Stop 500 meters (1,640 feet) before the sanatorium to see the red rocks.

The Jeti-Oguz area is best known for its bright red sandstone rocks. Check out the Broken Heart, a large hill spliced in two. Legend says it represents the heart of a beautiful woman who died of sorrow after two suitors killed each other in a fight for her. The seven red cliffs at the end of the canyon are said to come from a king stealing the wife of another king. The king who lost his wife went to see a wise man and asked how to make the king-thief suffer as much as possible. After hesitating, the wise man recommended that he kill his former wife, letting the king-thief have a dead wife, but not a live one. At a funeral feast in the mountains a few days later, the king sat next to his former wife. As the last bulls were slaughtered, he drove a knife into his wife's heart. Blood flowed from her heart, carrying the seven bull carcasses and the king-murderer with it into the mountains and the valley. The seven bulls turned into seven mountains.

Where to Sleep

The **Jeti-Oguz sanatorium** (Tel: 93-7-19, 93-7-23), built in the 1930s, is a dank, crumbling cement block with poor service. However, it has a spectacular location, along a rushing river and right across from the red rocks, and still attracts quite a few local tourists in summer. The prices are corresponding low. A single room costs 170 som, a rather cold mineral water bath costs 25 som (the baths are open all night), and a swim in the pool is 25 som. There is also a massuese available.

Some of the yurts lining the road seem to offer sleeping space. There are many wonderful spots for camping. Follow the path listed below in What to Do. Within a half hour, you'll arrive at the first of many good camping sites.

The **Saidahmat Yurt Camp** (Tel: (03922) 28561) operates 7 kilometers (4 miles) beyond the resort, from late May until late August. $18/day includes accommodation and 3 meals.

Where to eat

If you stay at the sanatorium, they may or may not let you eat there. You might be better off feeding yourself at the yurts, cafes and shops just outside the sanatorium compound.

The sanatorium only provides meals to people staying for a while. A great family-owned cafe across the street, **Kokjaik Café** (recognizable by the front patio), serves fresh and tasty local food. It's open year-round and 24 hours in summer. They also have a decent selection of drinks, sweets and ice cream. They plan to make the building next door into a hotel.

Upon approaching the area, you'll pass several stands selling fresh honey. Beyond those, several yurts sell food, drink and koumiss. There is a good selection of shops and cafes at the end of the road, across from the sanatorium.

Transportation

In season, marshrutkis leave the sanatorium daily at 7 for **Bishkek**. There are also regular marshrutkis to the sanatorium from **Karakol**. Otherwise, get off at Jeti-Oguz village and hike, hitch or take a taxi the 12 kilometers (7.5 miles) to the gorge. In season, it should be pretty easy to get a ride.

What to Do

The sanatorium offers mineral baths, swims in the pool, massages, and other treatments.

Take a **hike through the canyon. Follow the path to the left, just before the guardhouse when entering the sanatorium complex. This leads to a rocky dirt road, passable by mountain bike. It's an easy path to follow, winding through the canyon and under pine-covered slopes, occasionally crossing the river over bridges made of tree trunks. The path emerges into a boulder-strewn field, then crosses the river one last time. At the fork in the road, going left will take you into the vast meadow of the Kok-Djaiyk valley, the Valley of the Flowers. Here you can rest while marveling at the sight of horses and cows running free. Continuing straight at the fork will take you to the summit. Another half hour walk from the end will take you to a waterfall. On summer weekends, quite a few cars come through the canyon and it's possible to hitch a ride. From the fork back to the sanatorium by foot takes about one hour and allows a nice view of the **seven red cliffs** standing sentinel at the end of the canyon.

The South Shore (Between Jeti-Oguz and Barskoon)

Just past the village of **Orgochor** (in the direction of Karakol) is a statue of two famous local men. Uluu oichul Cart ake was the leader of this region. Uluu oichul Tilekmat ake served as a diplomat to Kazakhstan, Russia and Uzbekistan.

The **Chon-Kyzyl-Suu** gorge is near the Chon-Kyzyl-Suu village. It means "big red water" and is named after the red rock that gave the river its red color. At the meeting of the Djili-Suu and Chon-Kyzyl-Suu rivers is a health resort with hot springs over 43 degrees Celsius (109 Farenheit). This is a good place to hike to see waterfalls and glaciers.

Kyzyl Suu is a large, active town with cafes, a market, and the Issyk-Kul sanatorium (in the lower part of town). It's a pleasant, vibrant place that might be worth spending some time in for those interesting in getting to know local life.

Nine kilometers from Saruu, in the direction of Karakol, is the marked turnoff to the **Balchak Mausoleum** and **Red Cave** (10 km or 6 miles away).

The **Djuuka gorge**, near Saruu village, 35 kilometers (21 miles) from Tamga is more than 50 kms (31 miles) long, 60% of which is covered by forest. At the meeting of the Djuuka and Djuukuchak rivers there are red rocks covered by grass. Six kilometers further on is a health resort. This is a good area for hiking to see mountain lakes. There are shops in the long, quiet village of Saruu as well as hot water springs and a radon pool. Here is also the marked turnoff to the **Ychdobo burial mound** (12 kilometers or 7.5 miles). The **Jyrgal Yurt Camp** (23 ul. Mamadjan; Tel: 0502-348002; 700 som/person, including 3 meals) can set up horse tours and treks to the Barskoon waterfall, Lake Djuku and glacier Djuku.

Darhan is a long, dusty village with lots of horse-drawn carts. In summer, residents busily prepare carts of apricots for shipment. There are shops here.

In **Ak-Terek**, a village 23 kilometers (14 miles) from Tamga, there is a small *stolovaya* (cafeteria), as well as fantastic, little-used beaches just beyond the village (towards Karakol).

Between **Chon-Zhargilchak** and **Kichi-Jargylchak** is a series of nice, remote beaches.

Between **Barskoon** and **Chon-Zhargilchak** (13 kilometers from Barskoon), in the direction of Karakol, is the **Edelweiss Pansionat** (Tel: (03946) 95130, 25130 or 0502-935187). Located in a remote area, right on the beach, it is a prime place for quiet relaxation. Beautiful bays and beaches nearby offer great potential for lakeside strolls. Friendly management. You can get off here from any marshrutka running along the south shore. If you don't have a car, bring some snacks or drinks along, as there is no nearby store. The season runs from early June through late October.

Barskoon

Most visitors come through Barskoon, a village six kilometers (3.7 miles) from Tamga, to visit the waterfall, located within the 30 kilometer (19 mile)-long Barskoon gorge. It is also the start of the road to the Kumtor mine, which an take you up to elevations of 3500-4000 meters (11,500-13,000 feet), and the site of a 9th-14th century ancient fortress (6.5 kilometers or 4 miles away).

Tamga

Phone code: 03946

Tamga used to be a thriving village, with an airport and a major military rest site. Now it's a quiet, green village, 135 kilometers (84 miles) from Balikchy and 90 kilometers (56 miles) from the Jeti-Oguz gorge. A short downhill walk from town will bring you to the lake. The area is a good place to begin treks into the nearby mountains.

Where to Sleep

Tamga Guesthouse (ul. Ozyornaya 3; Tel: 333; d-sasha@elcat. kg; http://kyrgyz-travel.com, when entering Tamga, take a right on the first street after the orchard. The house is on the left) is a compound (sleeping 40 people) around a beautiful fruit tree and flower garden. The rooms are simple but neat and the food is especially good. Shared outdoor toilets and showers with hot water. The owners have an associated travel agency (see Travel Agencies in Bishkek) and can set up hiking, horseback riding and biking trips into the surrounding canyons and mountains, even at short notice. The size of the compound can give it the feel of a hotel, and the prices are a bit high compared to similar accommodations. But it's a pleasant place to stop or to relax and recover from a wilderness adventure. Beds cost 8 euro/person, food is 7 euro per day (2 euro for breakfast, 2 for lunch, 3 for dinner; the 3 euro box lunch is enough to snack on through an entire day of activity). Horse rental is $10 plus $20 for a guide and his horse.

The sauna is a pricy 10 euro for 1-5 people, 20 euro for 5-10 people. Children under five are free; ages 5-12 pay 8 euro for accommodation and food.

Dzhekshenbek Shamiraliev of **Zhak-Travel** (Tel: 0517-73-85-59; 347, 200, in Bishkek: (0312) 420000) offers similar, but cheaper, accommodations to the Tamga Guesthouse. A place in the house, which accommodates 40, costs 200 som. It's on the main road when entering Tamga, on the left-hand side. He also organizes trekking, horseback riding, yurt stays and eagle hunting trips in the surrounding mountains. Check ahead because his guesthouse can fill up in high season.

There is still a working **sanatorium** (Tel: 95-2-28) in town, though it caters primarily to tour groups.

Transportation

A taxi from **Bishkek** costs 1200-1600 som and takes 4-5 hours.

Volodya (Tel: 0502 566689) is a careful and reliable driver that runs regularly between **Bishkek** and the southern shore (**Khaji-Say**, **Tamga** and elsewhere).

What to Do

The **Tamga gorge** contains the more than a thousand year old stone writings of Tamga-Tash.

Between **Khaji-Say** and **Tamga** are the **Skazka (fairytale) rocks**. To find them, when traveling from Khaji-Say, look for a small lake on your right. After the lake, the road turns sharply to the right. Just after that turn, take the road to the right.

TON REGION

Beyond Tosor are a couple of lodging options, **Pansionat Zhemchuzina** (kilometer marker 134 (from west) and 86 (from east) and **Turbaza Issyk-Kul)** though it's unclear whether they are still operating.

Tosor

Tosor is another undervisited lakeside resort option, home to the yurt camp **Altyn-Kum**, which offers full-board, hot showers, fishing and horseback riding in summer.

The monument to the Ton region offers a good place for a rest or picnic, looking out over the water.

At kilometer marker 114 (from Bokonbaevo), 106 (from Karakol) is a marked turnoff to the **Soogultu petroglyphs**, 12 kilometers (7.5 miles) off the main road.

**Khaji-Say

This beautiful, lakeshore village has all the needed tour amenities, and very few of the tourists. The population has decreased from 10,000 in Soviet times to about 2,000 today. But it remains among the best places on Issyk-Kul to lay on the beach in peace and quiet. A tourist information center (Tel: 92561 or Veniera at 92422; www.issyk-kul-info.kg) in a little blue wagon dishes out information on the region's attractions from 9 to 5 in summer. Lodging options include **Turbaza Altyk Jeek** (Tel: (03947) 92368; costs 300-500/night including food, open from mid-June), **Pansionat Salima** (with the two swans near the entrance; Tel: (034947) 92244), **Sanatoria Legenda** (Tel: (03947) 92366), and the very nice cottages on the hillside **Utes** (Tel: 92105). Lilya (Tel: 0543 915678) rents out rooms in her private home at ulitsa Garajnaya 18.

If these are full, other places to try include:

Agat (03947) 92366.

Buston, Yubileini, Riviera, Kulanov, Satkyn (03947) 42883, 43373.

A *lepushka* stand near the bus stop sells delicious, hot bread along the roadside. A bit futher along towards Karakol, a double staircase of

24 sets of 8 steps makes for an interesting climb and a nice view of the lake. There is a toilet at the bottom of the winding staircase, a little further than the double staircase.

Volodya (Tel: 0502 566689) is a careful and reliable driver who travels regularly between Bishkek and the southern shore (Khaji-Say, Tamga and elsewhere).

Ton

Ton is a small village outside of Bokonbaevo. Coming from Bokonbaevo, take a left at the fork for the village beach, a right to continue on. Beyond Ton, many kilometers of shoreline offer excellent camping opportunities. Other lodging options (in summer) include the CBT yurt camp **Altyn Bulak**, the **Pansionat Agat** (about 10 kilometers or six miles outside Bokonbaevo) and **Pansionat Yubilayni**.

Bokonbaevo

Pop: about 14,000; phone code: 03947

A bit removed from the lake, Bokonbaevo is not very interesting in itself. However, its eagle hunters make it one of the best stops on Issyk-Kul. And it's also a good base into the nearby mountains, as well as to sites on the southern lakeshore.

Where to Sleep

Hotel Rahat (ul. Atakana and Turusbekova; Tel: 91631, mobile: 0502 614864) is a clean, pleasant and simple place, offering rooms for 200 som per person. Hot showers are available.

CBT has homestays for 450/person/night; 180 som per lunch or dinner. Meerim's home (ul. S. Kalkanov 34; Tel: 91115) is acceptable, but not overly friendly.

Where to eat

Café Ardinkur, located in the old blue building behind the bus stop serves up cheap local fare, similar to the few other cafes on the main drag. You can eat for about 50 som.

Gulzar, just down from the Bishkek taxis, is a friendly place serving basic local food for about 30 som/portion.

Transportation

A marshrutka from Bokonbaevo to **Tamga** costs 50 som. Taxis and marshrutkis line up on the main street, near the central market. After 3 p.m., it can be difficult to find marshrutkis to **Bishkek**.

Other services

Bakit (ul. Salieva 30; Tel: 91312) is the CBT coordinator and can provide information about local lodging, transportation and attractions.

The **Altyn Oymok (Golden Thimble) (69/70 ul. Kyrgyzskaya; Tel: (Jyldyz) 91590 or 91412) souvenir shop has a nice collection of gifts and shyrdaks for sale, made with natural pigments. You can watch the artisans at work in the area surrounding the shop. By making a purchase at the shop, which was established as a community development project, you'll be supporting artisans from the surrounding area.

CBT provides various services, including hunting with an eagle (2000-3000 som per demonstration or 5500 som plus tour price to hunt in the wild), felt carpet making demonstration (600-1000 som), horse rental and horseback and trekking guides. They can also organize visits to yurts near Bokonbaevo (450 som/night per person plus 180 som for lunch or dinner).

A visit to **golden eagle hunter Sarumbai Zarnaev (ul. Aitmanbetova 28; Tel: (03947) 91320) is reason enough to journey to Bokonbaevo. One of the most experienced hunters, he has shown his talents to former Russian president Boris Yeltsin and Kazakh leader Nazarbaev. Now he takes tourists out for hunts (high season is October through March). Zarnaev only hunts wild animals. You won't see any rabbits set out for easy catching here. And even if you don't catch anything, the horseback ride offers amazing views, only enhanced by the sight of the eagles swooping down from the mountains in search of prey.

A marked turn-off shows the way to the **Kandobo ancient settlement** (4.5 kilometers away) and **Bel-Tam yurt camp** (14 kilometers or 9 miles away). There is a bus stand for hitching.

Ak-Suu is a pretty village, located at the base of mountains. **Burbut**, a little further east, is located in a green valley.

East of Kara-Koo, the road follows a ten kilometer (6 mile) mountain pass, devoid of civilization, that reaches 2,109 meters (6,919 feet). There is a pit toilet, and some great views, at the top of the pass. East of the pass is the turn off to the **Jaychu yurt camp**, five kilometers off the main road. There is a bus stand at the intersection for hitching.

Kara-Koo

A sizeable village with stores and a café. A marked turnoff leads the way to the **Ak-Bashi petroglyphs**, 18 kilometers (11 miles) off the main road, in the direction of the mountains. Further east, there is a **café** near the entrance to a mountain pass. From the café, you can see the red monument to Babak Baitir, built by slain politician Tynychbek Akmatbayev. Beyond this monument leads a 14-km (9 mile) rough road to the small Shor-Kol **salt or dead lake**, worth a float if you come in the summer and have transportation.

The dead lake is a secret, hidden little lake that propels one up like a bobber, much like the Dead Sea. To get there from Barbulak village (74 kilometers or 46 miles from Balikchy, at the Babak Baitir monument):
•Take a left at the fork.

- Take a right at the next fork (after passing a small white house on the right).
- Take a left at the fork with a blue sign. There is a yurt and house offering rooms for rent and a café.
- Follow the brown sign with an arrow to the left for 200 meters. Rooms are also available for rent here.

Although it's only 14 kilometers (9 miles) , the bumpy dirt road, opened in 2001, takes an hour to travel. At the lake, parking costs 50 som, a yurt stay is 150 som/night and a meal in a yurt costs 70-80 som. The swim season is from late June through September. There is very little shade, so bring a hat, long-sleeved shirt and sunscreen.

If you don't have your own transportation, you can find a taxi in Balikchy or Cholpon-Ata or try to hitch a ride from the turnoff onto the dirt road.

In the roadside village of **Karatala** you can find shops. **Karashar** is a small lakeside village. There is a pit toilet a little further east.

Ortuk

Ortuk is the first sizeable village after Balikchy. It has a long, flat beautiful beach with teal water and looks like a good place for lakeside camping. It also retains some interesting communist relics near the waterfront.

Between Ortuk and Balikchy (km 16 when coming from Balikchy) there is a white curb where you can park and water coming out of what looks like a shower. This is drinkable mineral water.

NARYN REGION

The drive from Balikchy to Kochkor starts out through miles and miles of dry, desolate land. Scrubby land leads to brown crenellations. At a sparkling reservoir, the pale blue water laps against bare brown hills. The road passes through a canyon then continues along a river to Kochkor.

Kochkor

Pop: around 16,000; phone code: 03535

Kochkor is a pleasant, leafy town overlooked by a ridge of snow-peaked mountains. First named Stolypin, after the Tsarist Prime Minister who promoted Russian colonization in Central Asia, the Bolsheviks named it Kochkorka after the revolution. It is populated by friendly, welcoming people, many of whom are shepherds. It is one of the best places to arrange a jailoo visit. A row of yurt-cafes is located in the center of town where you can watch (and even try) making koumiss (fermented mare's milk).

Where to Sleep

CBT (ul. Pionerksaya 22A (Tel: 03535 22355; 0502 427562)) offers a selection of homestays in and around Kochkor.

Where to Eat

Visit Café is one of the better places to eat in Kochkor.

What to Do

Much of the Kochkor area offers good **biking** opportunities. Balikchy to Kochkor could make a nice ride.

Kochkor is a good place to set off for trips to the *jailoo* as well as to learn about local crafts. It's promixity to Bishkek makes it easy for those with limited time.

Transportation

Taxis and marshrutkis leave from the central area, in between the bazaar and the row of yurts.

An early morning marshrutka leaves for **Bishkek** around 7:30.

Shared taxis to **Balikchy** cost 60 som and take about an hour. Marshrutkis to Balikchy run sporadically.

CBT (see Other Services below) charges 2200 som for transport to Son-Kul and back plus fee for idle days if driver waits and full lodging and board for driver. To go to Naryn via Son-Kul costs 3600 som plus idle fee for wait time and full room and board.

Kuban Mambetaliev, a taxi driver who was raised on the shores of Son-Kul, is a safe, friendly and helpful driver. He is a good option for trips to Naryn and especially Son-Kul. Unfortunately he doesn't have a phone, but you can find him at ulitsa Sh. Akmatova 27 (coming from the south, take a right from Orozbakov onto Shamen street, before the yurts. Then take the second right after the palace of culture, onto Akmatova). He speaks only Russian and Kyrgyz.

Other Services

The **Shepherd's Life** contact is Mayram Omurzakova (ulitsa Shamen 111, 1 km behind bazaar; Tel: 21423).

CBT is located at ul. Pionerksaya 22A (Tel: 03535 22355; 0502 427562). It offers a full range of homestays, jailoo visits, transportation and tours.

Jailoo Tourism Company (ul. Sagymbai Orozbakov 125-3; Tel: 21-116; 0502 735188, 0502 527708; asipajailoo@rambler.ru; www. jailoo.com.kg is located on the central square, near the bazaar.

If you need a good bath after your jailoo stay, visit the private *banya* at ulitsa Sh. Akmatova 27 (coming from the south, take a right from Orozbakov onto Shamen street, before the yurts. Then take the second right after the palace of culture, onto Akmatova). It costs 15 som.

Catch up on your email at ulitsa Isakeev 31 (Open 8 a.m. to 11 a.m. daily) or the Kyrgyz Telecom office (ul. Orozbakova 126; Open 11-8:30 Monday to Friday, 8:30-5:30 Sat-Sun).

Tuz

Thirty eight kilometers (24 miles) from Karakol, in the village of Tuz, you can visit the salt caves used by the sanatorium **Chon-Tuz (book through Bishkek office at ul. Sokolukskaya 3; Tel: (0312) 23-42-

31 or 23-94-41). The caves are said to cure asthma, allergies and other respiratory problems. A guide will lead you among the 5 kilometers of walkways through the chill caves (the temperature stays at nine degrees Celsius (48 Farenheit) year round), taking you to a ping-pong table, billiard room, video hall, small lake, sitting room, reading room and disco. It's a surreal, dark world inhabited by visitors primarily from Kazakhstan and Russia from 7 p.m. until morning. Entrance and a tour costs about 300 som. A simple room with two beds and a sink at the sanatorium costs 1,000 som/day, including meals. Tuz makes a good bike ride from Kochkor, or you can hire a taxi for 400 som round-trip. There is no public transportation.

Near Tuz

When departing from Tuz, take a right at the cemetery, then stop at an old building on the left, where a chute emerges from a rusted tank. Look at the top of the tank and you'll see water bubbling out. Light a match to it and a fire will burn.

Also nearby is the picturesque **Aragol Lake**, which is expected to dry up within five years.

Son-Kul

Son-Kul is the ideal place to live out cowboy fantasies. The long (29 kilometers long and 18 kilometers wide or 18 by 11 miles) and smooth lake is located between the Son-Kul, Moldo-Too and Boor-Albas mountain ranges. Mountain pastures, where shepherds set up yurts and live during the summer while their cattle graze, surround the lake, offering wide open, treeless spaces for horseback riding.

A local legend says that when Ormon Khan, a local khan, first saw the lake, he fined the local tribe forty horses because they had hidden such a beautiful place from him.

In the 1970s the Soviets wanted to drain the water from Son-Kul to send it to Uzbekistan. It was "barely saved," according to a local, due to the influence of Subaliev, first party secretary from Kochkor.

With 18 rivers flowing into it, Son-Kul is Kyrgyzstan's second largest lake. But unlike Lake Issyk-Kul, which resists freezing all year, Son-Kul is frozen from November to May. Due to the altitude (3016 meters or 9,895 feet) the area is chilly, even in summer. It's possible to swim in the lake, but it is cold. Bring some warm clothes for your visit.

Where to Sleep

Tourist firms open yurts on Son-Kul from July 1 to mid-September.

CBT/Shepard's Life yurts offer the best lodging and are the most popular option. Lodging costs 250 som for B&B, 100 som per meal. Animal rental is 70/hour (420/day) for a horse and 30/hour (200/day) for a donkey. Guides are available for 400 som/day (500 som, English-speaking) or 800 som/day on horseback (900 English speaking).

Where to Eat

Son-Kul has some of the cheapest and fresh *koumiss*, sold for as little as 20 cents a liter.

What to Do

Take a walk or a chilly swim, ride an animal along the shoreline or through the surroundings hills, visit a local shepherd, admire the view of the sky and stars.

Transportation

You can visit the lake as part of a tour, arrange transportation through CBT or hire a private driver in Naryn or Kochkor. There are four routes leading to the lake. From Son-Kul to **Kochkor** is 100 kilometers (62 miles) and 2.5 hours.

The Places of Kyrgyzstan – Son-Kul

I arrived at Lake Son-Kul by crossing over a mountain pass, the blue visible in the distant valley. We drove past a large herd of yaks, descended into a valley and across a flat, treeless plain. We continued past yurts, the round felt portable structures shepherds live in, signs advertising *koumiss* or fermented mare's milk, and cattle, toward the blue. At 3,016 meters (9,895 feet), Son-Kul is the second largest lake in Kyrgyzstan, wedged into a valley amidst the Tien-Shan mountains.

My driver took me to a yurt belonging to his relative, a member of the Community Based Tourism organization. From there, I could watch the lake shimmer under the setting sun. I dined on fresh fried fish and maneuvered by the light of kerosene lamps in the evening. When the sun descended, the sky turned into a planetarium, with stars glimmering and shooting across the inky, vast sky. I slept on a pile of mats atop of *shyrdaks* (felt carpets) sewn by the yurt owner's mother and fell asleep to the sound of wind over water combined with the noises of cows, horses, sheep, dogs and camel outside.

At 6 a.m. I awoke to the ringing of my alarm. I opened the felt flap door and stepped out into a bright layer of frost. The sun had already risen in a glowing, pale pink sky, but my hands still burned in the cold, crisp air. I looked around at the family camel standing tall and lonely, a cow peeing with a loud splash, and the animals, whose noises I'd heard all night, bunched into groups around the yurts. Mountains, soft and blue in the early morning light, ringed the plain.

After a breakfast of eggs, thick bread, jam, cream and tea, three French guests and I rented horses. Kanat guided us. We rode up into the hills, across them, and then down to a few yurts scattered near one of the 18 rivers feeding the lake.

Kanat stopped and entered a shepherd's yurt while we waited. "There is going to be a *toi* tomorrow," he said when he emerged. "The family is going to circumcise their three-year-old son."

A *toi* is the name for a variety of family celebrations held by the Kyrgyz. There can be *tois* for birthdays, anniversaries, circumcisions, a baby living through its first few weeks. *Tois* are often costly and an opportunity for a family to show their affluence. This family had asked Kanat to invite some acquaintances as he rode out of the valley.

Kanat said the family planned to kill a horse the next day to eat and would provide a cash prize for the winner of the horse games they'd organize. Every invited family would be expected to give a sheep, worth about $50.

Fifty dollars was a lot of money in an area where the average monthly income was around $100. "What if the family has some major expenses coming up and can't spare a sheep?" I asked.

"If they can't give a sheep now," he said, "then they'll be expected to give it in the fall or spring. But they have to give it at some time. They will then receive a sheep in return when they hold a *toi*."

It seemed like the *toi* would be a money-making event, and that those who held them frequently gathered substantial resources. An invitation was almost an order to go. Not attending would offend the host. At the same time, attending a *toi* was also an informal savings mechanism, ensuring the giver would receive a similar gift in the future.

Kanat said the circumcision would be done by an untrained cutter and without painkillers for the boy. He told me he'd once cut a boy himself.

"Don't you feel bad?" I asked, when he described how men hold the child's limbs down while the boy screams.

"What is there to feel bad about?" he asked, with a shrug of the shoulders. "They did it to me."

On the way back, as we neared the smooth lake, we stopped at his sister-in-law's yurt. She welcomed us inside and invited us to sit on mats in the small, dirty interior that smelled of smoke, wool and mutton. A chubby, red-faced baby slept soundly on a mat in the corner. I could hear its light breaths as its chest rose up and fell back down. Typical of the Kyrgyz tendency to share what they have with guests, even if they have very little, our hosts served us cups of *koumiss* and hunks of bread with fresh cream. The sour *koumiss* made my lips pucker, as did the strangeness of drinking horse milk.

When we left, the horses followed the path curving around the lake's edge. From the saddle, I looked down into patches of bright green moss visible through the clear water.

Lake Son-Kul is the place to act out cowboy fantasies. There, one can feel the joy of moving under a domed sky, across a vast, flat field, with nothing to run into or trip over. It's a place devoid of media, and artificial sound, where the horse and rider live in the same environment and race across it together. It's a place to stroll, leap, twirl and fly, surrounded by calm, clear waters, soothing grasses, and protective peaks.

Naryn

Pop: around 40,000; phone code: 03522.

Naryn means sunny in Mongolian. But that name doesn't prevent it from being the coldest town in Kyrgyzstan. The average January temperature is -17 degrees Celsius (1 Farenheit).

The long, narrow town (15 kilometers or 9 miles long and 1-2 kilometers or one mile wide) is situated on both banks of the Naryn River, the longest river in Kyrgyzstan.

It was founded as a fortified point on the trade route from Kashgar to the Chu River valley and became a city in 1927. In November 1920 it was the site of a battle between a group of White Russians led by two wealthy peasants from Tokmok and Naryn and the revolutionary communist soldiers. They captured the local Red Army commander and killed the local Party chairman before they were defeated ten days later. A memorial in Naryn commemorates those who died.

The population is almost entirely Kyrgyz. Animal herding dominates the economy and it's known as a good place for *shyrdaks*. Naryn now hosts one of three campuses of the University of Central Asia, the world's first internationally chartered higher education institution.

Where to Sleep

CBT (Ul. Lenina 33, apt. 8; Tel: 50865, 0772 689262; Fax: 50865; kubat-tour@mail.ru) has a network of homestays in Naryn. Lodging costs 350-450 som/night per person and 150 som per lunch or dinner.

Celestial Mountains Razzakova 42; Tel/Fax: 50412; celest@ infotel.kg; http://www.celestial.com.kg/about_us/accommodation/ guest_house.shtml) runs a guesthouse that is reputed to be quite comfortable. Rates of $30/single, $36 double, $42/triple and $13/ person in a yurt include breakfast and an evening meal.

Where to Eat

The best place to eat in Naryn is **Anarkul Café** (in the center of town, near the university and the government buildings), where you can find salads (year-round), *gulash*, and excellent *lagman*. Peace Corps volunteers translated the menu into English.

Café Adek (next to the drycleaners) is another option.

What to Do

There is a **museum** on ul. Moskovskaya (open 9-noon and 1-5), north of the eastern crossroads where you can see costumes and learn about Bolshevik hero Tabaldi Pudovkin Jukeev. The friendly and helpful staff will answer your questions about the area.

CBT (See Where to Sleep) offers maps and ideas for several independent **treks** around Naryn, ranging from four to seven hours.

Places of interest in the area include a **deer nursery** in Eki-Naryn (45 km or 28 miles away), a **horseback tour** to Echki-Bash (35 km or 22 miles away) and the hotsprings at **Jilyy-Suu**. See CBT for details.

Ask around for the café that does karaoke, a highlight of night-time entertainment.

Transportation

A taxi from Naryn to **Bishkek** takes six hours and costs 350-400 som.

CBT charges 1700 som for a taxi to **Tash-Rabat** (about three hours) plus 550 som per day wait time. CBT driver Talai is nice. The price difference compared to taxis at the station is worth it if you don't have the time, energy or language skills for hard bargaining. You also get the guarantee of a quality driver vetted by CBT. You might be able to find people to go with you and share expenses at the CBT offices.

A **CBT** taxi to Lake Son-Kul costs 2800 som round-trip via 32 serpentine and 3600 som via the Moldo-Ashuu pass. For both, if the driver waits for the return trip, a fee is added for idle time, as well as for full room and board.

Local taxis charge about 1000 som to **Tash-Rabat** plus 200 per night wait time.

The People of Kyrgyzstan – Naryn Taxi Driver

Talai and I set off in his beat-up Nissan for the 130-kilometer (80-mile) trip to Tash-Rabat, a fifteenth-century stone caravanserai. The inn, located in a remote valley not far from the Chinese border, used to accommodate travelers on the Silk Road. Talai, a driver for a community based tourism group, regularly made the trip between his home of Naryn and the Chinese border. He shuttled tourists to Tash-Rabat and towards Kashgar, following a road that was once a branch of the ancient Silk Road.

Huge trucks, loaded down with goods from China, crawled down the roads. Our small car was definitely in the minority. We could hear the rumble as a truck approached and our car shuddered as one came past.

"I'm fed up with those Chinese," Talai said.

I asked why.

"Their trucks carry up to 80 or 90 tons of goods, when our roads can handle only 40. They are ruining our roads."

He showed me how on the China to Kyrgyzstan side of the road, indentations from the heavy weight had turned the tar into two troughs. On the Kyrgyzstan to China side, where they returned empty, the road remained level. The indented tracks made the road slippery and caused countless accidents in the winter, he complained.

"We used to be able to travel on this road with our eyes closed," Talai said. "Now we can't even go with them open."

Not far outside of Naryn, a naked boy got up from where he was lying in the road, apparently drying off after a swim. Gripping his penis, he darted off to the shoulder of the road. We drove through rolling green-brown hills, virtually unpopulated, toward a ridge of snow-capped mountains. Off to the side, an eagle flapped its wide wings. A few villages punctuated the otherwise desolate road.

"I guess it's our government's fault," Talai continued. "I don't know where our White House (the term for the white Kyrgyz presidential office building) is looking and it scares me to think of it. The Chinese don't let our trucks into their country. We have to unload everything at the border and then their people take it to China. But the Chinese give a few dollars at the border and we let them in all the way to Bishkek."

He told me the government was thinking of setting up an unloading station at Ak-Bashy, the last sizeable town before the border. There, the Chinese could unload and Kyrgyz Kamazs (heavy-duty Russian trucks) would take the goods inland.

"If they made such an unloading station, then we'd have some work," Talai said. "Our drivers would have something to do. They'd build hotels and cafes and there would be work for unloaders."

I reminded him that if it took three Kyrgyz trucks to carry the goods from one Chinese truck, prices would go up. He didn't seem to care.

"I'd rather pay more for what I buy and have decent roads," he said.

As we drove, he pointed out each passing truck, most of which spewed black smoke, and told me whether it was Kyrgyz or Chinese and how many tons it was carrying. The giant Chinese trucks pulled two trailers behind them, stacked high with goods far above the cab. They moved at a snail's pace, taking three days to travel the 540 kilometers (335 miles) from the border to Bishkek. I couldn't imagine how they managed to control their speed on the downhill sections of the mountain passes.

We traveled in the dust through whitish yellow hills, a stark and lonely landscape, but lovely in its isolation. As the road alternated between dirt and asphalt, we rolled our windows up and down, sucking in the thick air involuntarily.

On the dirt sections, we kept the windows closed to keep out the dust, and in the meantime, baked in the sauna-like interior. Beads of sweat glistened on our dust-covered arms, necks and faces and I could taste the grains of sand in the back of my throat. In the hot, dry, and empty land, the little clay houses camouflaged into the landscape.

A little later, we stopped with the hood raised to allow the overheated car to cool. A giant truck slowed down and stopped. The driver talked to Talai, then continued on.

"What did he want?" I asked.

"He wanted to know if anything was wrong."

"Was he Chinese?" I asked.

"Yes," he smiled sheepishly between puffs of his cigarette.

"They aren't all bad," I said. And he nodded. He could accept them as workers and as people, if only they didn't ruin his roads in the process.

Other Services

The **CBT Naryn** Coordinator, Kubat Abdyldaev is very helpful. It's worth visiting their nice office at ul, Lenina 8, apt. 33 (Tel: 50865, 50895; 0502 689262). It offers internet for 30 som an hour, crafts for sale and you can make photocopies from a good selection of guidebooks on Kyrgyzstan, China and the Korkoram highway. There are photos and details of local guesthouses, a list of buses with times and prices, and details of four independent hikes you can take near Naryn. Bed and breakfasts cost 290 som/night in town, 250 in yurts, meals 90 som, a guide 420 som/day and a horse 420 som/day.

The **Shepherd's Life** coordinator is Marima Amankulova (ul. Balasagyn 14; across river, beyond museum, on right).

You can find **internet** services at 44 ul. Lenina.

Find both art and souvenirs at the **gallery** in the town center.

A store with a wide variety of the freshest products is located across the street from the Anarkul Café. Another high-quality store is located in the 64 block of apartments, the largest store, with a sizeable stairway up to the entry door.

Excursions from Naryn

A few places of note to visit near Naryn include:
- The large **animal bazaar** held on Sundays in **At-Bashy**. It is said to be the largest in Kyrgyzstan. Get there early to avoid the drunks. To get there from Naryn, take a taxi (70 som/person).
- Find the ruins of an old Kyrgyz fort and visit a new museum in **Koshoi Korgon** (adjacent to **Kara-Suu** village). The museum was funded by Askar Salymbebov, an owner of the Dordoi bazaar who hails from Kara-Suu. Entrance costs 40-50 som and English explanations are available. If it's closed, knock on the door of a neighboring house to find someone to open it. To get there from At-Bashy, take a taxi from the small bazaar (30 som/person).

The road from Naryn to Tash-Rabat is an old branch of the Silk Road route. It can be hot and dusty in the summer, with the return road indented by heavy Chinese trucks carrying goods to Bishkek markets. At the point at which the road widens significantly is where a military airstrip used to be located. While crossing the Kyzyl-Bel Pass, you'll have a view over the At-Bashy range.

**Tash Rabat

Seventeen kilometers (10.5 miles) off the road from Naryn to Torugart is the ancient stone caravanserai of Tash Rabat. Estimated to originate from the 10th or 11th century, trading caravans that used to travel through the surrounding mountains rested and worshipped there. During the time of either Tamerlane or Genghis Khan, Tash-Rabat offered caravans headed to and from China protection from both bandits and weather. Located in a lush and remote mountainous valley, it provides a sense unlike any other of what the conditions must have been like for commerce at that time.

The stone structure was restored in the 1980s and no one can seem to agree how many rooms it contains. One guidebook says 30, a worker at a nearby yurt insisted there are 32 ("it's not that hard to count," she said), while a local museum guide said there are 40 or 41. With half of it constructed in the hill, the interior is larger than it appears. Visitors can walk through the domed central chamber into the cold, dank remains of all of these rooms, including the khan's quarters. Entrance is 50 som.

Accommodation is available in yurts on the premises, which operate from June through September or through arrangement with **CBT** (see CBT Naryn). Sapyrbek Baike's yurt has been recommended. Basic meals and some souvenirs are available from the yurt owners. It's a good idea to bring some snacks to share.

A wonderful excursion by horse or foot is the eight kilometer (5 mile) hike to Lake Chatyr-Kul. This mountain lake, located on a plateau between the At-Bashy mountains and the Chinese border, is the highest sizeable lake in Krygyzstan, located at 3,530 meters (11,581 feet). It is 23 kilometers long by 11 kilometers wide (14 by 7 miles) and fed by 41 small rivers. To get there, you'll cross a 3,968 meter (13,018 foot) mountain pass, walk through limestone and quartz crags and pass silver rocks covered with orange-red lichen. The hike to the lake takes 4-4.5 hours from the Tash-Rabat yurt camp, about half that to return.

To get there, take a taxi from **Naryn** or **At-Bashy** (at least 300 som/person). From Tash-Rabat to Son-Kul is 250 kilometers (155 miles), or six hours.

The Places of Kyrgyzstan – Lake on the Roof

Early morning at Tash-Rabat, smoke from dung fires mixed with the morning mist; a rich smoky scent emanating from the felt yurts.

Just before eight, I set off with the yurt owner's eleven-year-old son to visit Lake Chatyr-Kul, which means the lake on the roof. At 3,530 meters (11,580 feet), it's the highest among Kyrgyzstan's four main alpine lakes. As we started our walk, the world looked green fresh and reborn and smelled like new grass.

I had seen the boy the previous night, his face red and chapped, riding into the yurt camp on a donkey. When he dismounted, the donkey took off, running and neighing across the valley, dropping its saddle on the way. Nazar took off after the runaway donkey, smiling as he ran, as though he'd been through that situation before.

"He'll probably become a shepherd," his mother told me. "He's good with animals."

When I'd asked for a guide up the mountain, I had expected an adult. When his mother told me she was sending Nazar with me, I didn't mind at first, figuring that if he wasn't with me, he'd probably be collecting dung. Later, his mother told me the father leads horse treks and the 11-year-old leads walking treks because the father considers it too far to walk.

In any case, I found myself with this child and his dog Dingo for the day. In his village, the school offers classes only in Kyrgyz. So I exhausted his Russian vocabulary in the first five minutes. This led us into a long and comfortable silence for most of the day, punctuated by one-word questions - tired? OK? backpack? pretty?

We started with a one-hour walk along the valley, beside a clear, tinkling creek. Along the way, we passed several yurts and many herds of cattle - cows, horses and sheep. We walked through a herd of yaks with large, scraggly bodies, narrow, scruffy necks, small heads and shaggy tails. They raised their large, pink nostrils as they looked at me, grunted like a person snoring, and went back to chewing the grass.

We headed toward a wall of rock that rose straight up before us. Along the path, we slipped on cow manure. There were no dried patties near the camp. They had all been collected for fires.

Nazar was respectful and accommodating, leading at a moderate pace, frequently asking if I was OK or if he could take my backpack.

Once I reassumed him I was OK, he walked with a relaxed, comfortable stride, seemingly at home in his environment.

We enjoyed a silent walk through remote, beautiful nature, hearing only the sound of the creek. Escarpments of rock rose above us, with rock replacing grass the higher we went. As we moved higher up, the sounds of the wind, the panting dog, chirping birds and squeaking groundhogs were added to the repertoire. The groundhogs ran across the mountains, stood up next to their holes, and scampered inside. They seemed to have poorly developed self-preservation instincts, announcing their presence with a high-pitched squeal.

Three hours later, we were headed up a long, tough ascent. When we took a break at a stream, Nazar doused his head with cold water. He lifted his round, wind-chapped face, sighing with pleasure as the water dripped from his hair. We heard thunder as a pack of horses ran across the mountain.

As we continued toward the 3,968 meter (13,018 foot) peak, the animals disappeared. I heard that mountain sheep existed, but I didn't see any. I began to feel light-headed, weak, short of breath and headachy. As a couple of French tourists caught up to us, I heard shallow, panting breaths and the clink clink of walking sticks against the rocks.

The path through the limestone and quartz peaks felt like a staircase to the clouds and we started to become level with them. The clouds looked like cotton balls floating in a blue soup. The air seemed to shimmer and move, to become visible.

In four hours and 15 minutes, we made it to the Ag Zo peak, where the Chatyr-Kul lake suddenly opened out before us. The lake was long, still, shallow (someone told me it gets no deeper than 20 meters or 65 feet), like a large puddle drying up on a plateau. Melting snow from the surrounding peaks fed it.

This was the Ak Sai valley, the border area between Kyrgyzstan and China. The only signs of civilization were a few tiny houses in the distance, which I was told belonged to the border patrol. Bare mountains and snowy peaks rose on the opposite side.

When we first began our walk, I was exhilarated by the beauty. When the climb became painful and my legs turned to rubber, I understood why locals think Westerners are strange for considering mountain treks fun. Upon reaching the summit, I felt joy, relief, and pride. Suddenly the pain was worth the chance to feel the accomplishment of the summit and to take in the breathtaking scene.

A permit is technically required to descend to the lake, since it is in the border zone. Nazar's mother had told me no one would touch me if I went there. But adding another two hours to the trek didn't seem worth it. A good eight hours of walking was enough for one day.

Nazar collapsed at the ridge, made of shards of rock, and fell asleep while I continued up to the peak for a better look at the lake. A cold wind blew steadily, leading us back down within an hour. Looking out at the contrast between rock, green valley, lake and sky, it was hard to believe that one of the valleys we had walked through was the site of one of Kyrgyzstan's ugliest incidents, the Urkun tragedy. Sheid valley means place where innocent people died. In 1916, anti-tsarist revolts took place across Central Asia following Russia's decision to draft non-Slavs into the army to fight against Germany. At least 100,000 people are believed to have been killed during the following Russian repression or died trying to reach China over mountain passes exceeding 3,000 meters (9,842 feet).

In that valley, a group of Kyrgyz trying to escape to China were shot by the Russians and buried in a mass grave. The exiles who made it across the border now live in the Kara-Kyrgyzski autonomous region, where they can see a daily Kyrgyz-Chinese news broadcast.

On our return trip, we passed two Kyrgyz women on horseback. I had begun to feel the loneliness of the empty landscape and was relieved to come across people. A little later, a teenage girl passed us, giving a young boy a ride on the back of a horse. Nearing five o'clock, it was time for the cattle, as well as the humans, to head home. I saw cows cavorting down the mountain towards their homes. I never knew how cows could run until I came to Kyrgyzstan. On the opposite mount, horses whinnied as they raced across the mountain, a thunder from the ground to answer the thunder we'd heard from the sky.

If you choose to take the rough trip from Naryn to Jalalabat, via **Kazarman**, one highlight would be seeing **Saimaluu-Tash**, an open-air stone gallery, located on a plateau in the Ferghana Range. It's one of the largest collections of petroglyphs in Kyrgyzstan from the Bronze and early Iron Age. It can be accessed by hiking or horse from mid-July to mid-August. CBT in Kazarman (ul. Bekten 36; Tel: 03738 41253; 0777 224063; reservation@cbtkyrgyzstan.kg, cbttours@mail.ru, a_rajiev@yahoo.com) can assist with lodgings and transportation. From Kazarman, a taxi to **Naryn** is 400-450 som/person and to **Jalalabat** is 600 som/person.

Crossing into China

In order to cross into China via the **Torugart pass** (200 kilometers or 124 miles from Naryn), travelers need special guarantee letters that they will be served by Kyrgyz and Chinese travel agenies. Otherwise, they can't cross the border, even if they have both visas. Compared to the Erkechtam pass near Osh, this crossing is more expensive, but less time consuming.

TALAS REGION

The Talas region is known as being the site of the one of the greatest battles in Eurasian history. In 751 Turks and Arabs, together with Tibetan assistance, drove the Tang Chinese army out of Central Asia, introducing Islam and changing the direction of Central Asian history. Evidence of inhabitation exists from the Stone Age and several places within the region display rock drawings as old as 2000 BC. It is also known as the reported birthplace of the mythical Kyrgyz national hero, Manas.

Today the Talas Region is cut off from its traditional orientation to Taraz, Kazakhstan by an international border. Vast mountains separate Talas from the rest of Kyrgyzstan.

It is an agricultural region, known for growing beans they refer to as "white gold" (exported to Turkey, Bulgaria and other countries) and a traditional Kyrgyz culture. Despite being a very affordable place to spend some time, it receives relatively few tourists and is a good place to visit Kyrgyz cultural monuments and to observe local life.

Talas

Pop: around 60,000 and growing; Phone code: 3422.

Talas is one of the most traditional Kyrgyz areas. When the Russians arrived in 1864, Talas was a small village. In 1877 the town of about 100 houses was founded as Dmitrovskoye. It's now the regional center, but retains a small-town feel.

Where to Sleep

The **Hotel Talant** (on the corner of ul Frunze and ul. Panfilova, in the 59th microregion; Tel: 43386) is the plushest pad in town. The hotel's 10 rooms come in only *half-luks* (800 som) and *luks* (1200 som). The only difference is that the *luks* rooms have two rooms. The rooms are clean and modern, with private bath, hot water, TV and breakfast included in price. There is an attached café and a seminar room. The hotel is a 5-10 minute walk to the center.

CBT (Tel: 52919) has four guesthouses in town. It's best to book first through the CBT office in Bishkek or contact the Talas coordinator. If you can't, contact the guesthouses directly, but it's good to make sure the coordinator knows you are there so CBT gets its 15% share, needed for the organization's sustainability. The coordinator, Turdubek Aiyilchiev, runs a guesthouse at ul. Yuzhnaya 76 (Tel: 52919; 0502-

643466; cbt_talas@mail.ru; to get there, head south on Frunze, take a right on Kirova, take a left on Yuzhnaya (the last street before Kirova bends and heads into fields. It's the last house on the right). His wife Kishim is a fantastic cook and the family is friendly and welcoming. I had the best *koumiss* I've tried in Kyrgyzstan at their home.) Other homes include Sabira's (1 edelweiss; ul. Sadobaya 197), and Aisulu's (2 edelweiss, ul. Frunze 282; Tel: 52947, 0502-404801. Muhiya (2 edelweiss, ul. Yuzhnaya 37; Tel: 53784) only accepts guests in groups of 3 or more. 250 to 420 som/night.

Talas has plenty of standard, Soviet-block **apartments for rent**, often used by Turks coming to Talas to buy beans. Contact Mira at 0502-696158 or 0502-880679 or Makil at 42651.

The **Hotel Erlan** (ul. Saragulova; Tel: 52497) is located smack in the center and its five clean rooms with private baths offer good value at 150 som/person or 300 per room. A 400-som room comes with a double bed and TV. Hot water available, friendly staff.

There is a hotel at ul. Lenina 149 (Tel: 42718), near the bus stop, four kilometers from the town center. It appears to be a private home.

Though it is located 20 kilometers (12 miles) from central Talas, in Orguchkor village, the Picassoesque **Baibol (Tel: 42146; 0502-493100, baiboltravel@yahoo.com to get there from Talas take a taxi (150-200 som), or get on a marshrutka headed to Baikay-Ata or Kirovka and ask to get off at Baibol) tourist complex is probably the most pleasant place in the area to stay. Fruit trees, hearty vegetable gardens, colorful flowers and creatively designed fountains cover the expansive grounds, where guests can stay either in an authentic yurt, or in a remodeled home. An elderly gentleman started the development of this area during his time as a Farmer-Hero of the Soviet Union. He still roams the premises and his friendly descendants can do everything from cook fantastic meals to arrange tours in the area and play traditional instruments. Lodging costs 300 som/night/person, breakfast 50 som and dinner 100 som.

The Places of Kyrgyzstan – Talas

I quickly felt at home living in my yurt near Talas. Each evening after work I changed into comfortable clothes. Then, while it was still light, I sat on a hillside swing and read with a view of the garden, flowers and mountains. I watched Saiagul picking strawberries. She was one of the pre-teen girls in the family who often served dinner. Her companion, Makpal, gathered armfuls of round, red tomatoes and long, green cucumbers.

Adil, the white-bearded patriarch of the family and Farmer-Hero of the Soviet Union, strolled up and down the cobblestone path, leaning on a cane and wearing a tall, traditional felt kalpak hat. "I have a feeling the air is cleaner higher up," he'd tell me, then welcome me to eat apples and strawberries right off the trees and plants. The sweet scents of apples, strawberries, flowers and vine vegetables mixed in the air.

Talas is one of the most indigenous areas in all of Kyrgyzstan. The population is overwhelmingly Kyrgyz, people speak primarily in Kyrgyz and signs, which are usually bilingual, are sometimes in Kyrgyz only. I heard traditional names I hadn't heard elsewhere and I was surprised to find *koumiss*, usually found in yurts along mountain roads, sold everywhere, even in cafes in the center of town.

The girls would call me to dinner at eight. The main course was always accompanied by apples, watermelon, home-baked bread, sliced tomatoes and cucumbers from the garden, homemade raspberry or blackcurrant jam, and smooth, sweet cream made from cow's milk.

It surprised me to never see beans on the table because everyone in the area rowed them. But no one seemed to eat them. When I asked to buy some of the famous Talas beans, people would invariably ask: To eat them? I wasn't sure what other purpose there could be, besides perhaps planting them like the locals do.

After an unsuccessful search at the market, I managed to buy one kilo of beans from a trader who buys beans locally and exports them to Russia. One evening, by special request, my guesthouse cooked me some beans for dinner. They didn't seem to know what to do with them – how to spice them, what to mix with them. Plain boiled red beans appeared on my plate, but I still liked them.

After dark in the dining room I would work on my computer or make international phone calls with my cellular phone, appreciating the wonders of technology that can connect Urgochkor to another continent. Returning to the yurt for bed, my steps along the cobblestones rang out in the silent night.

Talas is a remote region. At the time I visited, one paved road led to Talas town, but it involved going through Kazakhstan, which required a Kazakh visa. The second option followed a series of hairpin turns and a 3,586 meter (11,765 foot) ascent, then crossed another mountain pass on a dirt road. The low green mountain landscape is scattered with boulders. White snow stripes cover nearby peaks and yurts dot the area; shepherds taking advantage of endless green snacks for the herds of cows, goats and sheep.

Each evening, I'd fall asleep on a soft pile of mats with a view of the stars through my yurt's open roof. In the middle of nowhere, I felt I was in the center of the universe.

Where to Eat

Almaz (ulitsa Lenina, near school 4) is a quiet café with slow service and little selection, but good food. The whole roasted chicken is a good bet. In autumn, the second floor is used for weddings and other celebrations.

Koktom is the restaurant/café/shop/pharmacy across from the White House. The restaurant on the second floor has some of the best food in Talas, as well as a refreshingly pleasant atmosphere that seems to be removed from town. The bird chirp that calls the waiter is a nice touch. The large menu includes salads, soups and main courses. A meal runs 100-150 som. In summer, enjoy a drink under colorful tents with a creek running through the nearby garden.

Insan (ul. Saragulova, near the post office) is another café with a regular following and reliable quality. It serves both national and European meals in a clean, simple, pleasant area. Fried lagman is popular among the locals. The blini with sour cream are also nice. Expect to spend around 75 som for a meal.

Kiremet, a café located next to the Telegraph office on Saragulova street, serves primarily national food and is one of the better cafes in Talas. The chicken (*okorochka*) is good. You can eat for 50-100 som.

Restaurant Eles (Tel: 52417; open daily until midnight) is similar to Kontom, with nicely set tables, magenta furniture amidst pink walls and a wide selection of salads, soups and mains. From the White House, walk straight down Saragula. It's on the left, near the intersection with Manas, the entrance covered in greenery.

A new shopping center opened next to the market with a restaurant that's on the road to becoming popular.

Another quality restaurant is located opposite ATF Bank (see Other Services), on the corner block opposite the market. Besides Koktom, it's the only other place with an outdoor summer area. The restaurant is on the second floor, above the food shop.

What to Do

The last 65 kilometers (40 miles) to Talas and most of the road further on is paved, offering good opportunities for **bicycling**.

In summer, it is possible to stop at one of the yurts along the Talas-Bishkek road to try some *koumiss*, *borsook* and a bit of mutton. A snack costs around 20 som.

Locals like to relax at **Nulde lake**, 10-15 kilometers (6-9 miles) from Talas along the road near the bus station that turns off from the main road.

If you are in the area in the fall (after the harvest is sold and paid for) and can snag an invitation to a **toi** (various family celebrations on which a family can spend one third to one half of its income) you'll have a unique opportunity to see the events that life revolve around.

The **local market** attracts people from within a 20 kilometer (12 mile) radius. The early Sunday morning **cattle market** and the weekend **cattle fodder market** can also be interesting places to visit.

Transportation

The street names are marked with new Kyrgyz names, but people still refer to streets by their old Soviet names.

There are two routes to Talas from **Bishkek**. A paved road runs via Kazakhstan (400 kilometers or 250 miles), but you need a Kazakh visia. Most travel through Kyrgyzstan (300 kilometers or 185 miles), over two mountains and an unpaved section of road, though it's expected to be upgraded by 2008. 10-15 marshrutkis run per day, charging 300 som per person and taking 5-5.5 hours. Shared taxis are also plentiful, charging 400 som/passenger and going a bit faster than marshrutkis. To order a taxi to or from Talas, try: Nurland (careful driver with Audi 100 and seatbelts that function, even in back), Chingis, Talant (Tel: 0502 731992) or Baktigul (Tel: 0502 430717).

The station is four kilometers from central Talas, on Lenina street. Marshrutkis and shared taxis frequently run between the station and the bazaar.

You can find shared taxis to **Bishkek** at the central bazaar, as well as at the station.

Reach the only taxi by order service by dialing 155. These taxis are more expensive than those picked up on the street, charging about 60 som within the city.

If you choose to stay at Baibol, Baktiar (Tel: 0502-854349) will chauffer you to and from town for 150 som each way. Or you can find shared taxis from the station for 20-30 som/person.

Marshrutkis to **Kirovka** begin running at 8 a.m. and cost 30 som. Find them at the station.

The nearest train station is about two hours away, in the village of **Maimak**, where **Russia**-bound trains make a two-minute stop.

CBT can arrange drivers to go almost anywhere in the region, at a cost of 8 som per kilometer.

Hitchhiking is fairly easy within the Talas region, though the standard precautions apply.

Other Services

The **RDS-Elet project** (ul. Frunze 208; Tel: 52836, 0502449270 (Omurzak); Fax: 53893; sllpctls@ktnet.kg; to the left of the Komtom restaurant is an auto school, with government-looking blue panels on the building. Inside, on the first floor, you'll find the RDC-Elet office on the right) is probably the most useful place to contact before or upon coming to town. At the office, you can see photos of different sights in Talas and get ideas and contacts for activities, lodging and transport. Omurzak Churmukov is especially helpful. Open from 8:30 to 5 Monday through Friday.

The **CBT** office in Talas seemed a bit more disorganized during my visit than others I'd patronized. The former coordinator ran off with the CBT funds and disappeared, leaving the group without a formal office. The homestays continued to operate and the tourism services may have improved by time of publication. If you want to plan a longer excursion, it's best to first get some ideas from the Bishkek CBT office and ask them to book it through the Talas branch.

Internet is available at the central post office for 30 som/hour, 2 som per page for printouts. Open until 8 p.m. A high-speed connection can be found for the same price, but only from 3-8 p.m. at the **Center**

Internet Borbory (to the right of the Telephon office on Frunze, 2nd floor; Tel: 42314).

You can change money at one of several **exchange** booths near the central market. ATF Bank (ul. Sarigulova 59; http://www.atfbank.kg/branch/talas/) changes dollars only; no travelers checks.

The tourist firm **Noyon (Нойон)** is located on the first floor of the Intourist Hotel, on ulitsa Riskulova 1 (Tel: 53582, 53579; firmanoion@rambler.ru). It offers treks to lake Sary-Chelek and to Besh-Tash national park. They seem to work frequently with tourists coming from Kazakhstan and can arrange pick-ups at the border.

Near Talas

Locals argue that if you haen't been to the **Manas Complex (museum is open until 5, grounds until 8), you haven't been to Talas. The complex was created in 1995 to celebrate a millennium of Manas and renovated in 2003. Many locals visit on Nooruz in March and on Independence Day.

The highlight is the mausoleum to national epic hero Manas. It is thought to have been built in 1334 and is pictured on the back of 20-som notes. Made of baked bricks with clay mortar, a double dome tops it. It is dedicated to "the most glorious of women Kenizek-Khatun," the daughter of the regional governor. Legend says that Manas' wife Kanikei purposefully ordered a false inscription in order to keep his enemies from desecrating his body.

Manas was said to weigh 10 kilograms (22 pounds) at birth. At age 15 he became khan of the Kyrgyz people. He married a Tajik woman at age 30 and she changed her name to Kanikei, meaning legal wife of the khan. He grew to 2.5 meters tall and was reputed to have superhuman strength. When his mother gave birth to him, she dipped him in water. That water served as a protective shield. However, the spot where her hands held him remained dry and was vulnerable. He died from a stab to the back.

Near the mausoleum is a Hun period burial group and the ruins of an 8th-9th century stone fortress. A six meter (20 foot) bronze statue of Manas stands on an 18-meter (59 foot) pedestal in the rose garden. You can have your fortune told in the yurt.

In the museum, most exhibits are labeled in Kyrgyz, with some Russian. The guides recite a memorized speech.

The complex is located in Tasharik village. Marshrutkis to Manas Ordo leave from the bazaar and the bus station or you can catch a taxi from Talas.

Besh Tash (5 rocks) national park is a popular destination and probably the most beautiful canyon in the Talas area. The road through the park takes you along a rapid crystal clear river, and into mountain valleys dotted with yurts. **Baibol** (see above) has a guesthouse in Besh Tash at similar prices as does Turdubek Aiyilchiev of **CBT** Talas.

If you want to go far into the park, it's best to take a Niva or Moskvich. The rocky and rough road will give an owner of a foreign car a heart attack. From the Talas bazaar, it's 17 kilometers (10.5 miles) to the park entrance. To reach the lake, travel another 40 kilometers (25 miles), then walk for a kilometer or two. To get there, you can hire transport (talk with drivers at market or station, or CBT can organize transport for 8 som/km). Marshrutkis travel from the central bazaar to Besh Tash village (near the entrance). You can try hitchhiking from there. The road is dirt and sometimes rocky, but it is passable by mountain bike. Entrance costs 40 som per vehicle plus 80 som per person. The best time is visit is May, when the valleys are green and flowering, or in winter to go sledding.

About 20 kilometers (12 miles) to the northeast of Talas are three petroglyph sites: **Kulan Sai**, **Kurgan Tash** and **Terek Sai**.

Just before the village of **Orguchkor**, about 18 kilometers (11 miles) from Talas, is a pretty river and a road into the forest. It makes a nice spot for a picnic or quiet relaxation.

The monument in between the villages of Orguchkor and Orlovka was built by a wealthy Talas native, now living in Osh, in memory of his father, who was a *datka*, or respected man.

In the village of Orlovka is a **museum** to the life and work of **Theodore Hertzen**, an artist and book illustrator. He is most well known for his series of more than 200 linocuts based on the Manas epic. His paintings have been used by many authors, including Chingis Aitmatov, to illustrate their works. Arrive early in the morning, or easier, ask Daniyar at Baibol to set up a visit for you.

Just under 70 kilometers (43 miles) from Talas is the **Kirovskaya Reservoir**, a popular and beautiful place to relax and swim. Two resorts along the shore (one is named Edelweiss) offer food and beverage, water toys, umbrellas and a place to swim. Kazakh visitors visit the reservoir in large number, making this the only place in the Talas region where one can hear Russian spoken as lingua franca. It's best to visit early in summer, when water levels are high. Bring flip-flops for the muddy shore and base. Take a bus to Kirovka/Kyzyl-Adir, then hire a taxi.

In **Aral** one can see rocks in a variety of interesting shapes.

Sheker

Population: 4,300.

Sheker, which means sweet, is located 104 kilometers (64 miles) from Talas. In this sweet little village, the pride of Kyrgyzstan, author Chingis Aimatov was born. Contact Gulipa Kazieva (ul. A. Zhakipbekova 14; skymanas2000@netzero.net) for lodging, meals and tours. Her relative, Medina Kilichbaeva, is an excellent guide.

The town sees tourists an average of three to four times per season. Since visitors are still so rare, the community is happy to share information with those who take the trouble to get there.

What to Do

Gulipa Kazieva can organize a tour of the city. Among the places you might visit are:

- A small white **mosque** from the 18th-19th century and a newer one next to it.
- A garden of statues, called **Aitmatov's museum**. The sculptures represent heroes from Aitmatov's work.
- **Jer Uy cave**, which contains the remains of a nobleman, his wife and servants, underground routes and ancient ornaments.
- The **museum** in the House of Culture. You'll have to find the keeper to open it for you.
- Meet Aitmatov's distant relatives and view some of the people and places mentioned in his books. This includes Sultan Murat, from <u>Year of the Crane</u>, the cave where Ismail hid and

the place where Ismail ran from the police to Kazakhstan, from Face to Face.

Transportation

Sheker is best reached by taking a bus from Talas to Kirovka, then another bus for a one hour ride to Sheker (25 som).

Maimak has a good river for swimming. It's also the site of the nearest train station to Talas.

**Kok Sai

Population: 5,000.

Kok Sai is one of the prettier villages in the Talas region, with the region's highest mountain peak, 4,482 meter (14,704 foot) Manas, towering over it. A short trek by horse gets you out of civilization and into legend-filled mountains. The RDS-Elet coordinator, Zheksen Abduriov, served as the director of the former sanatorium for 15 years. He and other villagers enthusiastically welcome visitors. This is a nice place to go to see real Kyrgyz village life, to get off the tourist path, and to support a local community eager to share its resources and stories.

Where to Stay

See Zheksen Abduriov (ask anyone and you'll be led to his house) for guesthouse services. A night in the guesthouse costs 250 som. Breakfast/tea is 59, lunch and dinner 90.

What to Do

A horseback ride into the surrounding country is a must. Contact Zheksen for horses and guides. A guide costs 350 som/day. Horses run 50 som/hour or 250 som/day.
You might visit some of the local legend sites:
•A bowl-shaped rock called the **Dragon Stone**. Once, a boy went out, wearing his ring that protected him from harm. He was missing for several days. The girl who loved him went out looking for him. From the opposite mountain, she used an

arrow to shoot the dragon who lived in the rock. She cut the dragon open and found his ring inside.

• A rock with two trees planted on either side, growing towards each other. This reputedly marks the place where Oljobay lived with his love Kashijan, who was his mother's sister. Oljobay's uncle was against the union because Oljobay was poor. The fact that they lived together was shameful, as a woman's virginity was checked by examining the sheets after a wedding night. When the uncle found them, he killed Oljobay and brought his body to Naryn. He removed Oljobay's heart and dug a grave. Kashijan asked her brother permission to say goodbye to Oljobay for the last time. She went into the grave with him, kissed him and said she couldn't live without him. While still in the grave, she stabbed herself in the chest. The Uncle declared he wouldn't allow them to lie together in the same grave. But the two trees growing together in this spot shows that God brought them together.

• A rock shaped like a resting camel. In the 17th or 18th century, Kalmaks stole a local girl to be the 2nd, 3rd or 10th wife of an old khan. She was only 14 or 15 and he was old. She didn't like him and thought of her family and homeland every day. When she had a chance, she ran away on a camel. They came after her. She and the camel fell into the river and drowned. The baby camel that had been with them remained, waiting for its mother, lying by the river's edge and crying. God turned it into a rock.

Transportation

A 6:45 a.m. bus leaves daily for **Bishkek**, via Kazakhstan. Buses leave regularly for **Kirovka/Kyzyl-Adir**.

Kirovka (Kyzyl-Adir)

Kirovka is a hot and dusty place in summer. It's interesting for bustling Kyrgyz traders at the large Saturday bazaar, and as a departure point for the water reservoir, which makes a nice swimming hole in summer.

Transportation

Buses leave for **Kok Sai** at 8:30, 10:30, 12, 3:30, and 5. A ticket costs 30 som.. Shared taxis are located near the bazaar. They cost 40 som per place.

Marshrutkis to **Bishkek** (via Kazakhstan) depart every hour from 8:30 to 8:30. 170 som.

Marshrutkis to **Talas** leave every hour from 8 to 5. 30 som. To **Orguchkor** it's 22 som and takes one hour.

A taxi to the beach at the **Kirovskaya reservoir** costs 100-200 som.

SARY-CHELEK BIOSPHERE RESERVE

Sary-Chelek is a pearl of Kyrygzstan, difficult to get to but if you have the time, well-worth the hassle. The greenish-blue mirror-like lake is surrounded by steep slopes of silver fir, myrtle and pine trees. Among the 34 mammal, 160 bird and over 1000 plant species are species found nowhere else on the planet. The mountain air is so sweet from the dew, flowers and herbs that breathing it is like drinking juice, with a different taste in each spot.

The lake is 7.5 kilometers (4.7 miles) long and varies from 350 to 1500 meters (1150 to 4900 feet) wide. The lake is up to 234 meters (768 feet) deep.

Fishing is allowed in rivers feeding the lake, but not in the lake itself. Camping, swimming and hunting are all prohibited. However, sometimes there is a man offering rides on a small boat. And the area offers fantastic hiking opportunities – ranging from a few hours to several day treks going as far as the town of Talas.

The 24,000 hectare (59,305 acre) Sary-Chelek reserve was founded in 1959. In 1978, a UNESCO resolution gave it the status of a "biosphere reserve" and it was included in the international network of biosphere reserves.

Several villages near the lake serve as bases for visitors. The closest to the lake is Arkit, which is located within the reserve.

Where to Sleep

Various tour companies offer lodging in the Sary-Chelek area. It's fairly easy to find lodging with a local family in the village of Arkit. They can also set up horseback rides, treks, and meals. **Berubai Chuketaev** charges 250 som/night. **Sultan Chuketaev** (Tel: (92) 136; you have to order the phone call via telegram from Kerben) charges less and organizes great horse trips.

Where to Eat

Bring supplies or arrange meals with local families.

What to Do

When you enter the park you'll need to register. You pay the entrance fee when you go to the lake. The fee is 60 som per car, 20 som per Kyrgyz citizen, and 860 som per foreigner.

If you happen to have an inner tube with you, the river running through Arkit seems to offer great **tubing** possibilities.

Visit the Thursday **market** at Kara Jyrach, where cattle, honey and walnuts are sold.

Take a **horseback ride** through the villages and into nature. Ask locals for how to arrange horses.

Transportation

A bus leaves from **Caravan** to Arkit at 5 p.m. daily, returning to Caravan in the morning. The trip takes 2.5-3 hours.

From the Western station in **Bishkek** you can also catch a taxi directly to **Sary-Chelek**. Aijibek (Tel: 0502 518128) will make the round-trip for 5600 for the car or 700/person/each way. If you want to pay for the entire car, you can visit in advance and make arrangements with the driver to pick you up directly from your lodgings.

Taxis can be hired from **Osh**, **Jalalabat** and **Tash-Kumyr**.

It takes four hours by car to travel to Arkit from **Karakul**. The road between Karakul and Tash-Kumyr is rough and bumpy, a stretch of mountains, rocks, curves and water reservoirs. From **Tash-Kumyr** on, the road is not bad and the scenery – a blue river with white rapids running through a valley and red clay fairy-like chimneystacks – is striking.

JALAL-ABAD REGION

Jalalabat

Pop: Around 75,000; Phone code: 3722

Jalalabat is the administrative center of Jalalabat oblast in the southwest of Kyrgyzstan, near the Uzbek border. Jalalabat is famous for its natural resources – healing mineral springs, vineyard, flowers, fruits, vegetables and nuts. Patients from India, China, Afghanistan and Central Asia have come to the mineral hot springs since the 10th century. The waters were believed to cure leprosy. Nowadays, Jalalabat bottled mineral water (carbonated and with a heavy mineral taste) is sold throughout the country.

Where to Sleep

The **Hotel Kutbolson** (on the mountain overlooking town, in the *kurort* (health resort); Tel: 25711, 25294; 55813, 56712, 55296) is located in the Kut-Bolsun sanatorium rest area. Rooms are neat and clean, furnished with simple but comfortable wooden furniture and include a TV, fridge, bathroom with almost hot water and a decent breakfast (only served at 8). The showers strangely don't have curtains, the service can be Soviet and even with the heat, it's still a bit chilly in winter. But it's a quiet and restful place, a 15 minute taxi ride from the center. Ask for a room on the right-side of the hall for a beautiful view (with balcony) over the city and valley. Single 1100 som, lux 2500-3000 som.

**Community Based Tourism (ulitsa Toktogul 3-20; Tel: 3-19-62; mobile 0502 376602 or 0502284164; Fax: 559331; Open 9-6 Monday-Sunday in summer; 9-5 Monday-Friday and 9-2 Saturday and Sunday in winter). From the bazaar, walk on ulitsa Lenina to Toktogul, turn right, the office is on the second crossroad on the left. In winter, there are three options available ranging from 350-450 som/person/night. In summer, there are 15 options. The homestay of Muhtabar Nurmatova is a bit out of town, but is a very pleasant house and the food is some of the best available in Kyrgyzstan.

Ludmila Ykovlevna (Tel: 4-13-04) helps out her daughter, a CBT member, rent out a small but cozy one-room **apartment** for 350 som a night. It's a good bet in the winter, sleeping two, with central heat plus an electric heater. Ludmila is also willing to provide dinner, for 60-90 som a night, even for single guests, though the quality of the food is variable. Ludmila is religious and prefers not to rent to unmarried couples.

Navruz Hotel (across from AKB Kyrgyzstan bank, in park area in town center: Tel: 20370, 20405(21). Excellent hotel with café, restaurant, bar, and beauty salon. In summer, ask for a room facing away from the summer café, to avoid the noise. Rooms cost 1305-1739 som, lux 2173-2607.

Manap (mikrorayon Sputnik, 10 mn by taxi from center; Tel: 53797). Good hotel, but in noisy, commercial area. Doubles 800 som, lux 900 som.

Tagai-Bii (across from Manap; Tel: 52187) is a mid-level hotel, with rooms from 300 som.

Gostinitza Mol-Mol (ulitsa Lenina, center of town; Tel: 55059). Old hotel, not recommended. 174-274 for a single, 333-418 for double, 552 with hot water.

Some guesthouses include:

Cholpon (Tel: 32587, 0502 571174

Alaiskiy region (Tel: 03234 21313)

Kerben-Aksy (ul. Baetova; Tel: 22371)

Zeine Jailoobaeva (ul. Taygaraeva 2, kv. 3; Tel: 43535; 0505 413430; scorpimeder@mail.ru)

Where to Eat

Café Shermuhamed (Шермухамед) (ulitsa Lenina, across from ATF Bank)) is a large, clean café with a vast selection of main dishes. They have an English menu. Soups range from 15-35 som, mains from 15-125, averaging 50-80.

The panoramic restaurant Ikram Aji (Икрам Ажи) (just outside the entrance of the *kurort*, often referred to as Panorama, open 12-midnight daily) is one of the best in town, combining a large menu, tasty food, and an expansive view overlooking the town and valley. It also has a nice dance floor for parties. Salads run 40-60 som, soups 50-80, mains 75-120, sides 10-15 and desserts 25-65. Open 12-12.

Café Erkindik (Эркиндик) (in the Smi (СМИ) center, across from the Navruz restaurant, near the *kalpak* monument that stands across from the parliament) is more of a place for a snack or people watching than a full meal. Very popular with Americans, especially Peace Corps volunteers, and locals looking to practice English, it is owned and operated by a friendly American named Terry. The pleasant, coffeehouse-like environment is unique in Jalalabat and it's a nice place to while away a few hours or an afternoon. The fresh-baked brownies aren't quite the same as the real version, but they are still a nice treat for the homesick. The bean burritos with tomato sauce and grated cheese can compete with Taco Bell's. There is an internet café in the basement (see Other Services). Open 9-6.

The Milk Café Dilshod (Кафе Молочная Дилшод), located across from the market and the railroad tracks, has soups, mains, salads, tvorog and blini, almost all under 30 som. For a milk café, they are surprisingly consistently out of milk.

Navruz rest center (in Toktogul park, off of ulitsa Lenina, near the Barpi theater and parliament; Tel: 5-63-38) has the nicest interior in Jalalabat. Frequented by well-off locals, the restaurant offers a large menu with European and national dishes and nice views of the park. But despite a large staff, the service is painfully slow. Salads 35-50, soups 15-40, milk products 7-25, mains 45-90, service 5% plus 15 som for music after 6 p.m.

There is a café on a main street that goes through the market (just next to the railroad tracks) that serves only lagman and shashlyk and is reputed to have the town's best lagman.

Ask locals to guide you to the little pub that brews its own beer and has a nice outdoor area in summer.

What to Do

Most visitors come to Jalal-Abad to visit the *kurort*, or health resort. Most are locals coming for treatment for their illnesses. The Sanatorium (open daily 8:30-4) takes walk-in customers for hot mineral water baths (30 som for locals, 50 for foreigners) and massages (available less frequently). Take a taxi from the city (100 som) or marshrutka 10 from ulitsa Lenina. The Sanatorium is located next to the Hotel Kutbolson. Go down several flights of stairs through a dingy building, walk through a hallway to another building, then turn left.

Walking down the road from the *kurort* to the town, you'll pass **Shor Bulak** on the right, where stairs lead down to a warm-water stream.

There are pretty Asian gates on the edge of town, on the way towards Bazar Korgon. Nearby is a statue of the Kyrgyz hero Kurmanbek.

The **Barpi Theater** (in the central park) was restored by several international organizations and puts on regular concerts. Locals say that concerts that cost 100 som are significantly better quality than those that cost 30 som. These productions are a fun way to see local entertainment, but the quality is more like a high school performance than a professional concert.

In nearby **Kara-Alma** is a good swimming river.

The Traditions of Kyrgyzstan – Khurban-Eid

The Muslim celebration of Khurban-Eid, or *Eid al-Adha* is a national holiday and a day off work. The first Eid, commemorating the fast of Ramadan, had taken place a few months earlier. Khurban-Eid is the second Eid, commemorating Ibrahim's willingness to sacrifice his son on Allah's orders. In 2005, it was celebrated over a three day weekend. Many traveled to villages to visit their relatives. The holiday emphasizes visiting one's parents first, then relatives and friends. Those who lost a relative during the past year sacrifice an animal (usually a sheep) on Khurban-Eid and share the meat with the poor.

On the morning of the holiday, people commonly visit the cemetery. Women aren't allowed to go to for a burial, but they can visit. The rest of the day is spent remembering those who passed away, giving away food and *plov* (rice fried in lamb fat with meat, carrots and onions) to friends, relatives, and the poor, and visiting friends and neighbors.

A cool fog covered the quiet city, the air cool against my skin. During the 20-minute walk into town, I spoke with Victor, my Russian landlady's husband, who I'd met along the way. He was going to check out what was happening in town. On the way, he stopped several times to shake the hands of his acquaintances and to wish them a happy holiday. "It's not a holiday for me," he said. "I'm Russian Orthodox."

Victor, a 56-year-old Russian, told me that his parents came from Samara, Russia, with their three children in 1944. They were escaping the wartime famine. Victor was the only child in his family born in Jalalabat.

He said many Russians used to live in the Jalalabat region, but most left ("ran" in his words) in 1990, when the Soviet Union came apart. I saw few Russians in Jalalabat and I heard more Kyrgyz and Uzbek speech than Russian.

"Why didn't you run away?" I asked.

"Because I had a job and an apartment and a family."

Based on the number of hands he shook on the way, he seemed to be on good terms with his neighbors. But he said he's often the only Russian at work in a group of ten and that the ethnic tensions can make relations difficult.

He has worked as a bus driver since Communist times, driving a route between Jalalabat and Lenin village, 40 kilometers (25 miles) away. Victor said that for him, life was only now getting hard.

"In the past, they used to give us a new bus every five years. But now I'm driving a 1990 bus. I pay rent and have to pay for all the repairs myself. There is a lot of competition now, with buses and taxis, especially since there are basically only two roads out of Jalalabat. In order to cover the rent and make a profit, a driver needs to work 30 days. But not many of these old buses can stand to be driven 30 days a month."

When I reached the center and separated from Victor, I found the central park buzzing with families and young people. Most of the women wore headscarves and long coats. The men wore short black jackets. People sat in pairs on swings, twirling around on a automated ride. Others stood in pairs on the four boat-shaped swings on an old swing set, using all their force to send the boats up as high as possible. The sound of their laughs, yells and excited chatter filled the air.

Knots of people gathered outside the yellow Barpi theater. The concert should have begun at three, but ticket holders had to wait outside until four before being let in.

The theater had been recently remodeled, funded by the U.S. Agency for International Development and a couple U.S. nonprofit organizations. Patrons walked through a carefully painted sea green lobby, into a fresh pink and white performance hall, where red velvet curtains hung over gold arched doorways. Despite the attractive surroundings, the theater remained unheated and retained its old bleacher-like seats on a scratched floor, like a school gymnasium.

The performance began. A series of self-conscious male singers performed, accompanied by a keyboard and an electric guitar. Above them, trios of red, orange, yellow, green and blue balloons hung from the ceiling with tinsel. The lights flashed on and off, seemingly dependent on how the lighting person felt at any particular moment. A little girl, no older than three, emerged from the audience and began to dance onstage. Dressed in a winter jacket and an ivory cap, she confidently shook her shoulders and hips to the Uzbek pop music like an experienced woman.

The audience was restless. People came in and out, talked, and got up to greet each other during the performance. No one sat in their assigned seat. A couple attendees used laser flashlights to point red dots on the singers' faces.

The hall only filled up 40 minutes after the concert started. At that time, young men began to gather in the back of the theater and formed a dance circle while a popular song was being sung. The audience attention and four video cameras turned to the back of the auditorium. A woman near the front turned around and smiled, flashing a row of pure gold teeth. The air smelled of dust, leather and chewing gum.

Not long afterwards, I had curious onlookers seated on either side of me – a 15-year-old and a slightly older and inebriated man. They took turns pulling on my sleeve and asking me questions – what was I doing there, was I married, did I have kids, did I know it wasn't normal to not have kids yet at my age, did I understand Uzbek, where did I live, did I like the concert, did I like it there.

"Everyone is looking at you now," the man on my right said. "They are wondering what you are doing." I knew their interest was friendly, based in the curiosity of something new. I continued to watch the concert and visit with my neighbors.

Neither neighbor was pleased with the concert, though the man was more disappointed than the teenager.

"How much did you pay?" he asked me.

"30 som (75 cents)."

"The good concerts cost 100 som ($2.50). This concert isn't very impressive and you can see, people are leaving."

He was right, people had started to leave in droves. The many empty seats stood out in the previously overfilled auditorium. No matter that people were still up there singing.

I thought back to when I first considered coming to Kyrgyzstan and I was told I could be posted in Jalalabat. I'd never heard of it. Looking on the map from across the ocean, it seemed like a remote, heavily Muslim and potentially unstable place. I remember thinking that alala in Jalalabat sounded a lot like Allah. I was nervous about the idea and hoped I'd be sent instead to the more Russified north.

I didn't integrate into the city in my two weeks there, but neither did I have any problems. Every day I walked the street alone, lived among locals in an apartment complex, and sat among them at a concert. It reminded me that no matter how frightening the idea of terrorism might be, I have to remember that terrorists are by far the minority. I saw that I could come, uninvited, to a Muslim festivity, and be greeted with acceptance and curiosity. I remembered that hiding behind my own culture and national border wouldn't do anything except increase misunderstanding and fear.

Transportation

Shared taxis to **Osh** cost 120-200 som per passenger, holding four passengers. If you want your own taxi, you can pay for all four seats. The trip takes about 1.5 hours. *Marshrutkis* start at 80 som.

Taxis for **Osh** and **Bishkek** line up in the parking lot across the street from Tsum.

Shared taxis to **Bazaar Korgon** cost 30 som per passenger and take about 30 minutes.

Call 123 to order a **taxi.** Furkat is a reliable local taxi driver, reachable on his mobile at 0502 366916.

Other Services

Starnet Internet Café is conveniently located on Lenin street, near the intersection with Toktogul (across the park from Kino Mir). Medium-speed internet use costs 30 som/hour. Starnet seems to avoid electrical outages better than some neighboring cafes.

Erkindik (Эркиндик) Internet Café, in the basement of the Erkindik Café, has a whole room full of computers. As long as the electricity is working, the connection is good and at 20 som per hour, competitively priced.

Bayel (Байэл) market, a wholesale market, is located on the edge of town, past the bus station.

**Arsalanbob

Pop: around 10,000; phone code: 3722

A gorgeous village, 99.9% Uzbek, set in a remote forest of walnut trees, the oldest and largest natural growth walnut forest in the world. Surrounded by waterfalls, mountain peaks and tree farms and populated by friendly people, this village is worth the effort of getting to. Take a few days if possible, stay in a homestay, and enjoy the views, the nature and the relaxation.

Where to Sleep

The **CBT** office in Arsalanbob (Tel: (0312) 44331; (0773) 342476; arsalanbob 2003@rambler.ru) is the best in Kyrgyzstan and has 14 member houses offering lodging for 300-350 som/night. Ibrigim Karimjanov (CBT house 6), a German teacher, offers a friendly homestay with a view overlooking a beautiful forest.

What to Do

Take a walk with one of the CBT guides. I used **Malik** and was pleased with his services. Another guide is Abdurazzok Koziboev (Tel: 5 47 98; abdurazzak f@mail.ru). Visit part of the 11,200 hectare (27,675 acre) natural growth **walnut forest**, the largest in the world, or the 200 meter (656 foot) **waterfall**, the tallest in Kyrgyzstan.

The CBT office is Arsalanbob is the best in Kyrgyzstan. A wide variety of activities are offered for all seasons – from hikes to horseback or donkey rides, to folklore or national tradition shows, to winter sleigh rides. There are also three-day trips by foot or horse to the Holy Lake. Porters and equipment are available.

Transportation

Arsalanbob is located three hours from **Jalalabat**. Transport options include marshrutkis and taxis, traveling via **Baazar Kurgon** (30-300 soms/person).

OSH REGION

The Osh Region makes up much of Kyrgyzstan's portion of the Fergana Valley, currently divided between Kyrgyzstan, Uzbekistan and Tajikistan.

The region has a long history, with people having settled around Osh's Suleiman mountain since the Bronze Age. In the fourth century BC, Alexander the Great was in the region. He made walnuts popular throughout the territory. By the end of the first millennium BC, Osh and the Fergana Valley were included in the Great Silk Road. In the 10th and 11th centuries, the Turkic Karakhanid empire built a capital at the nearby town of Uzgen, called Mavarannahr. From 1747 the Khokand khanate ruled all the Fergana valley.

During the time the Silk Road was used, Osh and the Fergana Valley were important stops. Coming from Kashgar in East Turkestan, the fertile plain would have provided travelers with plenty of food as well as the opportunity to purchase high-quality silk from Margilan.

In 1924, Stalin divided the Fergana Valley (the large Syr Darya river flood plain) between Kyrgyzstan, Uzbekistan, and Tajikistan, as it remains today. One theory is that Stalin ignored natural lines provided by rivers and mountain ranges, as well as areas defined by ethnicity or language because he wanted to discourage any of the areas from ever becoming independent countries. During Soviet times, the borders didn't influence local life very much. Only when the borders began to be taken seriously in 1991 were small Uzbek islands left within Kyrgyz territory. Uzbekistan's tendency to frequently close its borders has resulted in trade and movement difficulties for local residents.

A strong focus on cotton in the region and an inability to maintain irrigation has caused some farms to collapse. That and the lack of industry, plus local wages that can be as low as $30 a month for a full-time worker, have caused large-scale migration from the rural communities, especially to Russia.

The Osh region accounts for 14.6% of Kyrgyzstan's territory, but 24.5% of the population lives there. Historically, the Uzbeks lived mostly in the valley while the pastoral or nomadic Kyrgyz occupied the mountain slopes. As the Kyrgyz wanted to join others in the lowland for better work opportunities, tensions over space and housing erupted. The relative overcrowding, combined with a lack of housing and employment have led to some ethnic tensions, notably in 1990 in Uzgen.

Many in the Osh region have long felt that Bishkek has worked in the interests of northern Kyrgyzstan, though that perception has been decreasing since Kurmanbek Bakiyev assumed the presidency in 2005 with substantial assistance from the south.

The Osh region is the most fertile area of Kyrgyzstan. The mild climate ranges from an average of -4 degrees Celcius (25 Farenheit) in January to 26 degrees Celsius (79 Farenheit) in the summer.

Osh

Pop: Around 250,000; Phone code: 3222

The second largest urban area in Kyrgyzstan, Osh is often referred to as the southern capital. As early as the eighth century, Osh was known as a silk production site on the Silk Road. In the 10th to 12th centuries, medieval Osh was the third most important city in size and importance in the Fergana Valley, after Ahsiket and Kuba. The appearance of the Muslim religion dates from this date. In the fifteenth century, Osh belonged to the Timurid domain of Omar Khodzhi and Zakhreddin Babur. Babur, a famous poet and general, left recollections of Osh in a book. At that time, Suleiman-Too mountain was called Bara-Kukh, which means "a beautiful mount" or a "free lonely mountain" in Farsi. Its present name, meaning Solomon's mountain, appeared after the 16th century. The Russian Empire took over the city in 1876 when Russia beat out Britain in overwhelming the local khanates during the Great Game.

Today, it's a quiet and colorful small city surrounded by hills on three sides and located under a prominent holy peak. The river Ak-Bura divides the city in two. The over 3000-year-old city is home to Central Asia's largest open-air bazaar and the largest mosque in Kyrgyzstan. The fertile soil supports the growth of abundant fruits and vegetables and the diverse population (Uzbeks, Kyrgyz, Russians, Tajiks and others) is friendly. Today Osh is the starting point of the Pamir Highway, which travels via the Pamir Mountains to Khorog, Tajikistan.

Where to Sleep

The **TES center (ul. Sai-Boyu 5; Tel: 21548, 21651, 0502 505253, Fax: 56385; tes_centre@ktnet.kg) primarily houses international consultants and is often full, but it's worth calling ahead if you are looking for a comfortable room. Wooden decorated rooms with private baths are attractive. A common area holds a TV and computer with internet connection and makes it easy to meet the other guests. The 20-25 euro (30-35 for double) price includes a breakfast of eggs, sausage, cheese, yogurt, bread, juice, fruit and tea or coffee. Take a taxi at night, as the surrounding area is very dark.

The TLF Guesthouse (57 Suymbaeva; Tel: 55118; Fax: 55118) was originally opened by American missionaries and is now run by a geological society. It's located in a former kindergarten on the outskirts of the city. Rooms have individual heaters, a refrigerator, comfortable mattresses and a bathroom with hot water. It's not a bad place to stay, but still has the feeling of a remodeled kindergarten. Standard $25; luks $30; Apartment: $35/person.

Salima Sadikova and her husband Habib run a friendly and personable **guesthouse** in their family home (20 ulitsa Technicheskaya; Tel: 76712; mobile: 0772 008740, 0772 278032; 0777 807831; Farhad_2113@mail.ru). It's only a short walk from the center of town, the food is fantastic, and Habib is an expert outdoorsman and can organize trips to the surrounding mountains. $15/person/night lodging and breakfast. Delicious homecooked meals available for an extra charge. Some English spoken.

The **Alai Hotel** (ul. Kurmanjan-Datka 280; Tel: 57729) is centrally located and one of the cheapest options, but can be a hangout for unsavory characters.

Hotel Sara (ul. Kurmanjan-Datka, on right when going down Kurmanjan-Datka from Souleymane mountain toward mountain; Tel: 22559) has rooms from 215 som for a single (shared bath) to 1000 som for lux, including private bath and TV. Central location. Hot water available. Not the most friendly staff.

Kristall (near the bazaar, philharmonic and Suleiman mountain) has four doubles for 250-500 som, two singles with private bath for 800 som, and 14 suites. Breakfast costs 100 som extra.

The former hotel Intourist, now **Hotel Kyrgyzstan** (ul. Baylinova 1; Tel: 75614) is a grim-looking place, with rooms an overpriced $46-100.

Dolboor is a small, new five-room hotel, near Toktogul park and the new bridge. Doubles cost 500 som, half-luxs 1000 and luks 1500, breakfast included.

Jetigen (ul. Djim, Tel: 39910) has two complexes, each with five doubles. One is in the southeast part of the city, the other in Osh region. Rooms cost 700 som.

If you are looking for a longer-term apartment, Malika (Tel: 2-09-33) has several. Private flats run $20-25/night for the flat, sometimes per person. Some cheaper, more basic options include Arzikan (Tel: 28188) who had one good and one below average apartment, charging 300 som/night in summer and 350 between September and May; Nilufar (Tel: 30730), with good apartments for 500 som per 24 hours, one on Lenin and another on Zainebedinova.

The Places of Kyrgyzstan – Osh

The father of my host family, Habib, sat in his beat-up Niva in the driveway. He was in there with his friend, chatting, seeking protection and privacy from the wind. A heavy wind blew through the street, raising dust, covering Souleymane Mountain in the distance in a beige mist.

We'd started out the day with a breakfast of bread, fried eggs, sliced cucumbers and tomatoes and tea on the covered porch of my Uzbek host family's home. From our vantage point, we could look out at the roses growing in the courtyard, at the outdoor kitchen, where the mother, Salima, cooked in the summer time, and at two sides of their one-story U-shaped home.

As the day progressed, the pressure of increasing heat bore down upon us. One by one, family members drifted off, victims of lassitude in the stifling air. I resisted the urge to nap, but finally succumbed.

The weather in the evening seemed to try to make up for the discomforts of the day. The flowers in the home garden rocked wildly, a blanket of purple, white and red on a turbulent sea. Metal clanged as 11-year-old Lutfulo, Habib and Salima's son, did flips on the home training equipment and the neighbor's iron-sheeted roof rose and fell in the wind. The tree branches rocked as though they were flailing, the plastic sheet covering the wood pile hung on for life and a reddish glow from the sunset illuminated the bathroom and shower walls.

"A red sunset means that tomorrow will be hot," Salima, the matriarch, said.

Salima ran around sweeping, then sat quietly on the covered porch, her back against the wall. We could hear a faint bubbling from the outdoor stove and the scent of meat and dough. She got up to check on the pelmeni (a local version of tortellini) soup cooking, then raised her arms to the sky.

"What beautiful colors," she said, "orange and blue and yellow. And the rain is starting to fall."

It felt as though we were in a living museum, a museum of movement, where we had to hang on tight, but could still enjoy the colors, the wind and rain against our skins, and the welcoming warm yellow light from indoors.

The **Osh Guest House** (ul. Kirgistana 8, flat 48; Tel: 30629; Mobile: 0502008740; 0502 372322; 0502 883093; 0502 372311; oshguesthouse@hotbox.ru; www.oshguesthouse.hotbox.ru) offers beds at $4 a piece. Take bus 7 or a taxi from either the airport or the Uzbek-Kyrgyz border to "Magazin Aeropag." Go behind the Aeropag shop to three large apartment blocks. The Osh Guesthouse is the white building in the middle.

Other guesthouses include:

U Batirovix. (ul. Suinbaeva ½; Tel: 59336, 55351, 0502 359533) In the southeast part of the city, the guesthouse has four rooms (one with private bath) for $35 each, including breakfast.

U Zhukovwi, (Tel: 20072, 53197, 27576, 52338) $25/person including breakfast and dinner.

Golden House, $25-35 per person, including breakfast.

Taj-Mahal (ul. Zainabedinova 13; Tel: 39652); near the city center, 100m from central market

Aziza's Guesthouse (Tel: 0502 359336)

Barak Ata, (ul. Ibraimova 22/1; Tel: 55532, 0502 386972, 0502 447655) New guesthouse in outer region of city, private baths and hot water, rooms cost $40.

CBT (Tel: 0772 574940; osh_cbt@mail.ru) has B&Bs for 400-750 som/night.

New guesthouses on ul. Kyrgyzstana include **Sunrise** and **Elina**

Where to Eat

European:

**Odnozhdi (ulitsa Lenina, in between Lenin statue and stadium) is one of the city's newest and best cafes, offering modern décor, comfortable soft chairs, and good service. Korean and European entrees run 60-100 som, salads 50-70 som. Large cocktail list. A good option for a tasty, filling budget meal is the Korean *kuk-si* soup, with noodles, beef, eggs, vegetables and spices for 40 som. 15% service charge.

**Nazima (ul. Lenina, near the post office) is known for having the best roasted chicken in Osh (70 som). Service charge is 15 som per table, 25 som after 5 p.m.

**Rich Man (ul. Michurina; Tel: 24303) is an upscale European café, with comfortable seating and entrees from 60 som.

Russian:

There is a line of cafes on ulitsa Lenina, near the intersection with ul. Geologicheski. All are large, with indoor and outdoor seating areas. Don't plan for any important or intimate talks at night, when they blast the music, unless you're able to get a private room and close the door. Among these include **Café Vstrecha** (with reasonable, but not outstanding quality and value. The large fresh veggie platter with tomato, cucumber, onion and pickle is a good deal at 25 som.) and **Café Victoria** (better food than at Café Vstrecha, the fried trout and *ostri* salad are especially good; budget 150-200 som for dinner).

Russkaya Kuhnya (Русская Кухня) (ul. Israil Sulaimanov, between Kurmanjan Datka and Lenin) sells standard Russian dishes at reasonable prices. The chicken is quite good. You'll be charged five som for the pleasure of hearing the music blaring from the next door bar. Salads from 15-40 som, soups from 15 to 35, mains from 25-60.

Café Olymp (ul. Lenina, near intersection with ul. Bayalinov) only has three tables, each closed off by a curtain, and a similar number of entrees to choose from. The dishes and decorations are rather fancy, but the food is more expensive than average, the quality only decent, and the atmosphere somehow unpleasant. Salads range from 30-50, soups 28-46 and mains from 43-75.

Altyn Vodii (ul. Kurmanjan Datka, near intersection with Bayalinov (near AKB Bank)) is nothing special, but is an OK place for lunch. The *borsht* is among the best in Osh.

Café Ak-Bulak (Ак Булак) (located to the right of AKB bank on ulitsa Kurmanzhan Datka, near the intersection with Lomonosova; Open 8-24) opened in late 2004 and is a very good place for tasty food, a large selection and low prices. The pea soup and milk products (kasha, blini, etc.) are especially good. One can easily eat for 40 som.

Kyrgyz:

Café Ala-Too (ulitsa Kyrgyzstana and Zainamadinova) is one of the large, popular Kyrgyz restaurants lining Kyrgystan street. The food is fresh and reasonably priced. Best of all are the nice outdoor tables, where you can watch the action while you eat. Salads 25-60, soups 25-35, main dishes (including *dymlyma*, stewed meat with potatoes and vegetables) 25-80, drinks and alcohol. In 2006, a deputy was shot and killed here in one of the back, private rooms.

Café Sudarushka (Сударушка) (ul. Kurmanjan Datka, near intersection with Gapara Atieva, near the yurts below the mountain) serves up typical café food – stuffed peppers, meat, sausage, *borscht* and *shorpo*. In summer, big, frothy mugs of beer are served at outdoor tables. Soups 15-25 som, main dishes 20-60, salads 15-80.

Kashgar (ulitsa Kyrgyzstana, near the intersection with the street leading up from the footbridge across the river, south of Abdykadyrov) is a good quality café. The *mysa po kitaiski*, meat fried with vegetables on rice, is a winner.

A string of cafes with indoor and outdoor seating line ulitsa Kyrgyzstana, from Zainebedinonva north. These popular Kyrgyz cafes present a good chance to try different national dishes. Each café has a reputation for making one or two things well. Locals either have a favorite that they always frequent, or they choose where to eat based on what they feel like eating and who does the best job preparing it. **Café Turkmenistan is known for their *lagman*, **Ala-Too** for *samsi*, *lagman*, *uromoo* (similar to *manti*) and steak, and **Al Baraka** for *samsi*.

At **Café Kyrgyzstan** (ul. Kyrgyzstana), you can choose from standard tables or traditional Kyrgyz booths. The national dish *dymlyma*, made with meat, potatoes, carrots, peppers, onions and cabbage, is especially good, as are the *sirniki* (fried sweetened cottage cheese patties).

Zhibek Zholu (Жибек Жолу) (ul. Kyrgyzstana, near Zainebedinova) serves up meals for about 50 som per person, including options such as salads, *sirniki* and *blini*.

Café Gulnoza (ulitsa Kyrgyzstana) is a new, busy café with a chef from Kashgar. Food is mediocre.

Visit **Farhad chaikhana** (teahouse) on Nookatski podyom to glimpse at the local passion for *plov* and to see the teahouse culture in action. *Plov* is just about all that is served there, so bring any sides or special drinks you want.

Faiz is a *chaikhana* on the way to the airport, before Nurdor village, on the left. It's a place where bigwigs meet out of the eye of cityfolk.

The Traditions of Kyrgyzstan – *Chaikhana*

Despite the popularity of *chaikhanas*, or traditional teahouses in Osh, I'd never been to one because my host father told me only men were allowed there. He'd promised to get me permission to attend, but never did.

It turned out he was wrong. While the majority of clientele were men, women could go as well. I visited a teahouse for the first time, with my colleagues and my host family, just before leaving Kyrgyzstan.

The open square building surrounded a courtyard in the traditional Uzbek style. One must call ahead to reserve a room, say how many kilograms of *plov* (fried red rice with lamb's fat, lamb, carrots and spices) they want, and make a deposit. Each group eats in a private room, cut off from the others. And the *chaikhana* serves nothing but *plov* and tea. If you want anything else – juice, water, beer, salads, fruit – you have to bring it yourself.

Nevertheless, they do a very good business. The owners of this *chaikhana* had recently taken a $20,000 loan to expand their building.

When I walked around and peeped into the windows of the other rooms, I saw groups of men, soldiers, and middle-aged couples. Most of them sat on the floor, on cushions and pillows cupping round bowls of tea and eating the fatty *plov* from communal dishes. Our room, the largest, had a long table with chairs.

I wandered into the preparation room, where an old man in an Uzbek cap chopped meat, the knife falling onto the thick red mass with a thump. Heavyset men managed cooking the *plov* in giant semi-hemispherical vats called kazans. Like grilling in the U.S., making *plov* is an activity that men dominate and where one-upmanship is common. I could feel the heat from the stove, a cloud of warmth that cloaked everyone in the room. Red-cheeked women carried the steaming plates to the customers, the scent of fat and spices swirling upwards.

"They say that only men are able to successfully make this *plov*," Salima, my host mother, said. "When a woman makes it, it just doesn't turn out."

Salima's *plov* was the best food I'd eaten in Osh. I told her I liked her *plov* better. Her *plov* was light and seemed to melt in my mouth. I always started out with a small portion, expecting *plov* to be heavy, but would finish two or three bowls without fail. At the *chaikhana*, the fat made the *plov* heavy as one would expect. Tasty but filling, I couldn't enjoy the same quantity as I could with Salima's.

"My *plov* is a baby version," she said. "Since most of our foreign guests don't
like a lot of fat, we've adapted it. But at the *chaikhana*, this is the real thing."

Nothing better presents the local culture than eating real *plov* among the locals at a *chaikhana*.

Turkish:

Pegasus Café (at the central Aravanski intersection on ul. Kurmanjan Datka) is a round restaurant, surrounded by a canal. It serves Turkish food, including good bean soup and rice pudding.

Chinese:

**Restoran Huadali is a giant, often empty hall with an extensive menu in English, Russian and Chinese. It serves the best Chinese food in town, and while often cold in winter, it's a good place for parties. The menu includes humorous options, such as fried meat with banana in sour sweat sauce, fish in sour sweat sauce as a squirrel and fried meat with pignut. Salads range from 45-75 som, mains 120-280. Large portions.

Abadan Café (ul. Zainebedinova, off ul. Kyrgyzstana) serves Uighur and Chinese food. The stirfried beef and peppers, for 95 som, is good. 5% service charge.

Korean:

See **Café Odnozhdi** (above).

Restaurant Koreana (ulitsa Lenina, next door to New World Pizza; see below) has a large selection of salads (35-55 som), soups (20-45 som) and mains (most 60-80 som). There is a 10% service charge until 8 p.m., 15% after.

**Beli Lotus (same as above) has tasty Korean dishes, which include a main entrée of dog. The spicy fish salad and the Beli Lotus (chicken with peppers and tomatoes) are worth coming for. About 100 som for a meal.

Pizza:

The **California Café** (In between ul. Lenina and Kurmanjan Datka, near university and USAID office) tries hard to serve American-style pizza in a pleasant wooden dining room. But the selection is often sparse and the service spotty. The pizza is mediocre (lacking any tomato sauce), but the low price (100-130 som for a large pizza) attracts a regular crowd of locals and Peace Corps volunteers.

Pub Nirvana (ul. Osmonov; Microrayon Zapani Tel: 63784) is a popular foreigner's hangout, located at the edge of town and known for their burritos, pizzas and Chinese food. They frequently offer discounts and their special events, such as a Halloween bash, are worth attending. You can get there by *marshrutka* from Aravanski. A taxi from the center costs about 50 som.

The **Greenwood** (ulitsa Lenina, a little past the post office and just before the park Tel: 50514) offers beautiful views of surrounding trees during the day and a quiet, relaxing setting at night. It is most popular as a place for pizza and beer. Also recommended for onion soup. Salads 30-60, pizza 70-220 (200-800 grams).

New World Pizza (across from the Greenwood on ulitsa Lenina, Tel: 7-34-01) sells pizzas for 75, 150 and 200 som, spaghetti (50 som), burgers, cheeseburgers, and salads (20-70 som, ask for the mayo on the side). The pizzas are largely dough and cheese, but as one of the first pizzerias in the south of Kyrgyzstan, it's not bad. Delivery available. 10% service charge.

Georgian:

Buzeinep is a Georgian café owned by Koreans. It's located on ulitsa Lenina, to the right of the Lenin Statue (when facing it). The food is decent, and the outdoor forested patio is a popular disco area on summer evenings. But the management still hasn't figured out the meaning or practice of customer service.

Sweets:

Istanbul Pastahesi (intersection of ul. Lenina and Alisher Navoi) offers a fresh selection of tasty individual and full-sized cakes, *baklava* and other sweet honey products, and cookies. Sweets can be enjoyed on-site with a pot of tea or taken to go. The café also offers some snacks and breakfast, though the main draw is the sweets.

The best cakes in Osh (a good thing to bring if you are invited as a guest) can be found at **Slavyanka** (ul. Pioneerskaya, near the Procuratura, between Lenin and Kurmanzhan Datka, one street over fromthe main Aravanski intersection; Tel: 27966; 0502-143425).

Cafes **Islambek** (near Vstrecha Café) and **Atabek** (ulitsa Lenina, near the OSCE; Tel: 24062) are recommended.

Until the arrival of the **Narodni** (ul. Kyrgyzstana, near the old bus station/bazaar) chain, the closest thing to a Western supermarket was **Osh Market** (Aitieva 11; Tel: 2-54-23), near the central Aravanski intersection, located behind the round restaurant, Pegasus.

You can buy fresh, live chickens and turkeys at the **market**. Take marshrutkis 25 or 57 to the *Veshevoi rinok* and walk down the hill and to the right. The birds can be killed and defeathered nearby for a small fee.

Drinking and Dancing:

Stimorol (ul. Kurmanjan Datka, in Aravanski) is one of the most popular places for locals to gather outdoors for beer. Other good places to visit for a drink are: **Nirvana, Café Sudarushka** (in summer), **Tsarski Dvor** (ul. Lenina, across from Osh State University main campus, near Koreana restaurant) and **Rich Man Café**.

Stels nightclub (ulitsa Lenina, near the Lenin statue, across from the Chinese restaurant) is the nicest dance place in town, with multistoried platforms overlooking a dance floor. Rocking on Friday and Saturday nights, you'll find Kyrgyz youth and expatriates among the crowds. Entrance is 50 som for women, 100 for men. **Disco Club Tornado** (near the new bridge) is also popular.

Apple is a local karaoke place, hidden away at the back of the Drama Theater (go down the stairs in the back). You can choose from a wide selection of songs, reading the words at the bottom of the screen, as pictures of scantily dressed women flash by. Service is slow and it can be cold in winter, but can be a fun place to experience local culture. Drinks and snacks available. The pizza, especially mushroom, is good. 100-200 som/person.

What to Do

The main attraction for visitors to Osh is the towering and everpresent **Suleiman-Too (Solomon's throne) mountain, where King Solomon supposedly spent a night. To Central Asian Muslims it is the third most sacred place, after Mecca and Medina. Enter behind the silver dome off ulitsa Kurmanjan Datka, just past the Silk Road Museum. You may need to pay 3 som at the base of the hill. Ascend up the stairs to the viewing platform and the **Babur House**, the 16th century mosque built on the mountaintop. If you take off your shoes and enter the mosque, the attendant will read a prayer for a small donation. Continue down the steps on the other side of the mountain. You'll see a cemetery at the base. Commoners are buried toward the bottom, notables, including famous Kyrgyz singer Ryslai Abdikadirov (1941-1994), higher up. Local legend says the cemetery began when women were forced to jump off of the top of Suleiman if they cheated on their husbands. Their bodies were left in the area that is now the cemetery. At the **Chak-chak cave** you can insert your hand, pull out some rocks, and make a wish. People enter the **Tamchi Tamaar cave** to read prayers and touch a spring. Further along on your right you'll pass a sacred smooth rock, **Bel Bosh Tosh**, that people slide down. Slide down on the part of your body that hurts and it will be cured. Continue on toward the silver spaceship-like circle where the **Great Silk Road museum** (Open 9-1 and 2-6; entrance 10 som) was built within the mountain. The entrance was blasted out of the rock in 1978 and currently is home to a cafe. The exit is a natural cave. The museum artifacts aren't particularly interesting, but the structure of the cave makes it worth a visit. Especially surreal are the stuffed animals lining the steep staircase up through red rock. If you still have time and energy, descend to the road and follow it to the left back to Kurmanjan Datka. You can then visit the Silk Road Museum and the Alymbek Datka Museum (see below).

A **yurt city** at the base of Suleiman is a good place to try national food in summer, such as *beshbarmak*, or five fingers – a conglomeration of noodles, fat and meat.

There is an impressive collection of **petroglyphs** at the base of Suleiman mountain. Take a left before the arched entry leading up the mountain and you'll see mathematical sums, food, a snake and a home, among other Zoroastrian drawings along the face on the right. If you have trouble finding them, contact guide Sergei Nasarov (Tel: 03221 25934, troglos-man@mail.ru).

The **Silk Road historical-cultural museum** has a large collection of Kyrgyz historical and folk items, but the display is poorly lit and the explanations sparse (only in Kyrgyz and Russian). This museum would be best visited with a guide or at least with a local who could point out some interesting things. Entrance 50 for foreigners.

The **Alymbek Datka Museum similarly lacks explanation, but the novelty of a three-story yurt filled with bright weavings and fabrics makes up for any lack of understanding of what it might all mean. Datka, born in 1799, built nine streets in Osh with his own money, as well as nine canals, nine bridges and a medrassah for 120 students. He was killed in 1862 by the Khokand khan's forces. The first floor contains displays of Kyrgyz culture, the second information about the Datkas, and the third, the Kyrgyz legend of Manas. Open 9-12 and 1-6. Entrance 50 som for foreigners.

If you've got a racket and balls, you can play tennis at the riverside courts near the **Tes Center**. From the Tes Center, take the second small road to the left (if you reach the road that goes along the river, you've gone too far). Follow this back and the tennis courts are on the right. Usage of the courts costs 50 som per hour for asphalt (with lots of bumps and cracks) or 110 som per hour for clay (you have to water it before playing).

Take a walk through **Navoie Park**, the riverside park named after the Uzbek poet from the 14th-15th century. The fountain is a popular place to gather during the summer and on holidays.

Souvenirs can be found at **Saltanat** art salon (ul. Lenina 428; Tel: 2-42-59, 3-44-97, 0502 31 46 27; saltanat73@inbox.ru; open every day). The local artisanry includes ceramic plates from Rishtan city, Uzbekistan, Kyrgyz drawings, amulets and Kyrgyz symbols.

The **mosque** (on ul. Zanibadinova and Kyrgyzstan) is Kyrgyzstan's largest and a local landmark, though it is difficult for visitors to go inside.

Take a look at the large picture of Bakiyev on the central bridge for an example of personality politics. The portrait replaces one of Akayev, which was fire-bombed during the 2005 revolution.

The vast **central market, among the largest open-air markets in Central Asia is a mélange of colors, scents and sounds – a smorgasboard of activity for the senses. Bring your appetite to fill up on *lepushka* still warm from the oven, small potato dumplings, a varied of pickled salads and a variety of seasonal and colorful fresh fruits and vegetables.

Locals search for **wild mushrooms** on the hills of the southern side of the city.

Some nearby places to relax in summer include: **Salkintor** (a nice lake about a 15 minute walk from the end of marshrutka 9), **Mamakayeva** (1/2 hour walk at end of marshrutka 9), **Semiozierka** (in Yugovostok, ride to end of marshrutka 9 and walk 15 minutes). Marshrutka nine departs every 20 minutes. From the last stop, cross the little canal, go down the slope, along the path through a person's backyard and through a little gate. Go left. Cross the dam. Take a left to the Salkintor lake or follow the canal straight to other rest centers and Mamakaeva. A guesthouse along the canal (take a right at the stone wall, silver gate on the left) rents cottages for 100-150 som per person. Contact Emil at 0502-33-35-91.

Transportation

Between four and seven **flights per day travel between **Bishkek** and Osh. The one-hour flight is a spectacularly beautiful journey over snowy mountain peaks towering over clouds. With one-way tickets from $68, it's worth the trip just for the scenery. Check-in about 40 minutes before your flight. The flight takes approximately 50 minutes. The Osh airport has an Altyn air office, a pay toilet, an internet café, and a cheap café. Buy tickets at Kyrgyz Concept, other travel agencies, or directly at the airport. There are also flights available from **Osh** to **Moscow, Novosibirsk, St. Petersburg,** and **Urumqi**. For updated schedules, check http://eng.concept.kg/OshConcept/schedule.

Local marshrutkis cost 4 som, though due to high taxes, drivers are trying to raise the fare to 5 som. A seat in a marshrutka to **Kara-Suu** costs 10 som.

Taxis to **Kara-Suu** (20 som there, often 15 som back) and marshrutkis leave from ulitsa Kyrgyzstana, across the street from Alysh, near the intersection with Navoi.

Shared taxis to **Bishkek** fill up near the Kelecheck bazaar. The 730 kilometer (455 mile) journey takes about 10 hours and costs from 1200 som/person. Travel by *marshrutka* starts at 1000 som/person.

A taxi to the **airport** costs 120-150 som. There is also a *marshrutka* that goes to the airport. Kyrgyz Concept (see Other Services) will arrange a taxi to the airport for 350 som.

Comfortable rides on large buses to **Russia** can be arranged at ulitsa Lenina 712 (the Osh City Molochni Kombinat) (Tel: 03222) 5-74-42, 2-07-87; 0502-22-69-98. Buses depart Osh for Irkutsk, Ufa, Barnaul, Kurgan, Kamerovo, Kazan, Ulan Ude, Chelyabinsk, Krasnayarsk, Sverdlovsk, Novosibirsk, and Magnetogorsk.

You can order a taxi through taxi company **Fortuna** at telephone number 122. You'll be told the price over the phone, which will be higher than you'd pay with a cab off the street.

A shared taxi to **Uzgen** costs 60 som per passenger and takes 45-60 minutes. A *marshrutka* costs 40 som.

Travel to **Jalalabat** takes about 1.5 hours and costs 120-150 som in a shared taxi, 80 som by *marshrutka*.

Shared taxis to **Kyzyl-Kia** start at 150 som/person and take about 1.5 hours to cover the 90-100 kilometers (56-62 miles).

Distances:
Osh to Irkeshtam – 250 km (155 miles).
Osh to Peak Lenin – 310 km (193 miles).
Osh to Khorog – 735 km (457 miles).
Osh to Sary-Tash – 180 km (112 miles).

Other Services

Alysh (ul. Kyrgyzstana, near the intersection with Navaie; Tel: 76763) offers good quality aerobics classes. For 300 som a month, you can attend three classes a week. It's also a popular place for wrestlers. The modern facilities were built in 2004 by a deputy, rumored to be shady, who was later murdered. You can see his giant picture over the wrestling mat. It offers good quality for the price. Other options for aerobics include **Tamara in Aravanski, which has a good reputation, and **Nadezdha** in Osh region. The **post office** is located at 320 ulitsa Lenina, near the intersection with ul. Sulaimanov. It's open from Monday through Friday 8-5 and from 8-3 on Saturday. Greeting cards and other postal supplies are available.

Sama Muhtar (Сама Мухтар) drycleaners (Tel: 2-57-13) is located near the market. It costs 40 som to dryclean a pair of pants.

Dom Bwita (ulitsa Kyrgyzstana, near intersection with Abdykadyrov (the new bridge). When coming from the other side of the river, cross the bridge, take a left, and it's on the left, with several kiosks in front) is the Osh equivalent of a Univermag, but it's a rather poor substitute - dark, low vendor density, and with an atmosphere of an old, aging place. The first shop on the right sells some **crafts** and national products, though at higher prices than at the market or the Bishkek airport.

The TES center (5 ul. Sai Boyu; behind the stadium) has a small but very nice collection of **crafts and local goods** for sale at very reasonable prices. These include colorful boiled wool slippers, dried sweet melon, photo frames, and homemade peanut butter.

Kelecheck Plaza (On Alisher Navoi, west of ul. Kyrgyzstana) is the closest thing to a shopping center. **CBT** is located on the third floor.

Hollywood Cinema (ul. Lenina 428) is the newest theater, showing several shows a day on a large screen for 20 som. A long-time favorite is the DVD hall on the 3rd floor of the Dom Bwita (**Дом Быта**), where you can watch films from DVDs shown in a 20-seat auditorium.

AKB Kyrgyzstan (on the corner of Kurmanzhan Datka and Lomonosova, not far from the stadium) consistently offers the best exchange rates in Osh, probably in the country.

Inexim Bank (Ul. Kurmanjan Datka 287; Tel: 55254, 57029) also offers full banking services.

You can find **ATMs** in Osh at **Demir Bank** (ul. Kurmanjan Datka 180a) and **ATF Bank** (ul. Kyrgyzstana 73; Tel: 29137).

Internet club options include: **Mir.com** is run by an American and offers decent connections at low prices (from the stadium, walk straight uphill, passing AKB Kyrgyzstan on your right. Continue straight. You'll see a sign for Mir.com and an arrow pointing left on a store. Follow the arrows. Tel: 5-75-64); **Fox Internet Club** (Gapara Ativa 7-1 in Aravanski, between Kurmanjan Datka and Lenina; Open 9 a.m. to 10 p.m. daily) is more expensive than others at 35 som/hour, but the screens are large, computers new, connection fast, and you can use a flashcard there. The nearby **Spiderman** (ul. G. Aitieva 9A; Tel: 2-99-72) costs 25 som/hour but is slower and doesn't take flashcards. Other options include **Ipswich** (Ul. Lenina 428; Tel: 20515; 30 som/hour, open 24 hours) and **Arsenal** (ul. Aitieva 3-5; Tel: 21404; 25 som/hour)

Kyrgyz Concept (1 Bayalinova Street; Tel: 27991, 59450; Fax: 59450; osh@concept.kg) sells domestic and international air tickets and can also help with accommodations and travel. Staff speak English and are fairly reliable, though you sometimes have to follow up (and don't wait too long with a reserved ticket before buying!).

Munduz Tourist (1 Sovietskaya Street; Tel: 22276, 55500, 26655, 0502 302764; Fax: 55072, 56618; Munduz_tourist@hotmail.com, osh_munduz@netmail.kg) is a reliable local tourist firm. It can organize trekking, rafting, mountaineering (including Peak Lenin) and caving trips.

Contact the Rural Development Center (302 Lenin Street, Apt. 5; Tel: 74671; Fax: 22355; mobile: 0502 688013; sllpcosh@ktnet.kg, nurjan_kyz@yahoo.com) for information on how to custom-order a *shyrdak* from one of the affiliated handicraft groups.

The best **medical care** in Osh can be found at the *Oblastnaya vzroslaya* hospital. The **city hospital** (Tel: 22573) is on ulitsa Kurmanjan Datka. English-speaking staff are available at the **Center for Family Medicine** (ul. Zainabedinova 22A; Polyclinica 2, room 9, 2nd floor; Tel: 25420, 56991, 25375; Open Mondays and Thursdays from 8:30 to 12:30).

The People of Kyrgyzstan – A Stolen Bride

A smart, bright, energetic and hard-working person, Ainara impressed me with her energy and determination. She had a heart shaped face, long black hair and a bright smile. She'd completed her university studies with honors while working as a loan officer. Since I'd left Osh, she'd risen into a management role and one of her subordinates had named his newborn daughter after her.

"I hope that she will be like you," he told her.

During my time in Osh, several of my female friends and colleagues had been "stolen," the euphemism for the Kyrgyz tradition of kidnapping a woman for marriage. One was stolen while getting her hair done, another while walking home. Some women were stolen by strangers, others stolen by men they knew, but didn't want to marry. Occasionally it occurred with the consent of both parties, as a type of elopement. For each of these college-educated women, yearning to become professionals, it was a shock to fall victim to an ancient practice that has come back into vogue after the fall of Communism (when it was outlawed).

But I was especially shocked to hear, less than two months after I'd left Osh, it had happened to Ainara. Not only was she intelligent, trendy and modern, but she'd told me she had no interested in getting married.

During a visit to Osh, I met her for lunch at a small café in the marketplace, near the credit branch she managed, and asked her how it came about.

Kanatbek had been her friend for the past five years she told me, over the clink of dishes being picked up and set down again. She said he'd asked her repeatedly to marry him, but she didn't love him and she refused. At the time, she had been dating two other people.

One of the men she was seeing had offered to give her earrings, which is the sign of engagement. She refused, but agreed she might be ready in the spring.

On the evening she was stolen, she'd gotten together with Kanatbek and other mutual friends at a café. They asked her to go to the disco afterwards, then realized they had forgotten to bring money. So they proposed taking a taxi and stopping by Kanatbek's home on the way to pick up some money.

When they arrived at his house, the driver said he had another client and couldn't wait. So he drove off, and they all accompanied Kanatbek to his door. As Ainara got to the threshold, she was forced into the house, where his family was gathered, and they tried to put the scarf on her.

In the practice of wife stealing, the family of the groom plays an important role. Sometimes they know about the kidnapping ahead of time, helping to plan it. Other times, the groom may steal a woman on the spur of the moment and bring her back to his family without warning. In either case, as soon as the woman crosses the threshold, the females in the grooms family will surround the shocked girl, trying to put a scarf on her head. Once the scarf is on, she is considered married. While they don't put it on by force, the pressure is strong, especially from the elderly women the Kyrgyz girls have been raised to respect.

In this case, not only Kanatbek, his family and friends, but also the taxi driver had known about the kidnapping in advance.

"How did you react?" I asked her. The smell of our beef cutlets rose up, but I didn't have much of an appetite. They tasted dry, like cardboard.

"I cried," she said. "You can't imagine what it's like to be taken in by force and to suddenly be in that situation. We were friends and I didn't expect that from him at all."

She told me she refused the scarf at first. They put her in a room, by herself, for three or four hours, so she could think. I imagine she could hear all of the relatives through the wall.

Once a girl has been kidnapped, the groom's family is obliged to notify the girl's family. They will usually come to the groom's house immediately. Many families believe that once a girl is stolen, it is her fate to marry her kidnapper and that not doing so will bring shame on the family. Some more modern parents will support their daughters in leaving an undesirable husband. The decision must be made quickly though. Once the girl has spent a night at the groom's house, it's almost impossible to leave.

"My brother and his wife came and they told me I should make the decision myself," she said.

"Would they have supported you if you wanted to leave?" I asked.

"Yes." Her urban family was comparatively modern.

Then her mother arrived, very upset, and wanted to take Ainara home.

"My mother likes Kanatbek and she's told me in the past that he's a good man and asked why I didn't want to marry him. But she didn't want me to be married in this way."

"Why did you decide to agree?" I asked.

"If it had been a stranger, I definitely would have left, right away. Women didn't have that choice earlier. But now it's possible to refuse, and even to go to court. But what kept me there was the thought of what his grandmothers would think about me getting up and walking out. They would say I was bad. And because we had been friends for so long, I knew his mother and his grandmothers. When my mother came and tried to take me back, I saw his mother cry."

"Did you think about your boyfriend at the time?" I asked.

"Yes, I thought about everyone. I knew I didn't love Kanatbek, but I also knew that he was a good person, that he cared about me, and that he'd take good care of me. And seeing his mother crying had a strong impact on me."

Why, I wondered, would a middle-aged woman, educated in a large city under the Soviet system (in a time in which bride stealing was banned) believe that her son has the right to kidnap a person and make her his bride? Why would she want a daughter-in-law brought into the family by compulsion rather than by choice? Does she not realize that in her support of her son, she is supporting a tradition that puts her daughter at risk?

I had earlier spoken with a middle-aged Kyrgyz woman in Osh who had helped her son steal a wife by convincing the girl's mother to have her stay. Later, when her own daughter was stolen and the mother was devastated, it was her guilt at doing the same thing that made her give in to the kidnapper's mother. In effect, by helping their sons, they are sacrificing their daughters.

Kanatbek must have been confident of his ability to convince Ainara, because he and his family had already planned the wedding.

I asked Ainara what her life was like now, a few months after the kidnapping. She said that Kanatbek moved back from Kazakhstan, where he'd been working, to live with her. His mother is in Kazakhstan, so they have the apartment to themselves. She had to adjust to doing household chores, which she never did before, but said that her husband helps sometimes.

"Before, my brother's wife did everything. I would just help sometimes with the laundry on Sundays. But otherwise, after work, I was free. Now I have to cook and clean, but I've already gotten used to it."

She said that her boyfriend, who she expected to marry, was very upset. But emotionally, she seemed to have adjusted. She looked the same as always, dressed in trendy, tight-fitting clothing with matching accessories.

"Kanatbek isn't at all jealous, which is good," she said. "I can dress how I want to and go out with my friends."

She was about to enter her third month of pregnancy. I asked if she wanted to know the sex of the baby.

"No," she said. "And Kanatbek doesn't either. He just says he wants it to be as easy as possible for me."

That was unusually considerate compared to many local men, who expect their wives to reproduce and demand sons.

Ainara is as energetic and hardworking as always, planning to work as long as she can before the birth.

As a result of this crime, six months after our lunch date, a person would be born who never would have existed otherwise, as well as succeeding generations of people who never would have come into being. At the same time, the child that would have been born, had Ainara married her boyfriend, and all of his or her descendants, are now erased from possible existence. All due to one invitation to a disco on a cold January evening.

Kara-Suu

Pop: Around 20,000; phone code: 3232

Located just a few kilometers from Osh, Kara-Suu (meaning 'black water') is on the Kyrgyz-Uzbek border and a center of cross-border trade. A town with a similar name, Kara-Soo, is just across the border in Uzbekistan. Uzbek traders come to bring cheap Chinese goods back to Uzbekistan. Vendors from Osh stock up on the lower-priced goods at the Kara-Suu market. Besides the active trade, Kara-Suu is a dusty and dull town.

Where to Eat

Café Minutka (across from the central market) is to the right of another café by the same name. This one has wooden tables, an outdoor seating area, and delicious roasted chicken and *samsi* prepared in a tandoor.

Transportation

Marshrutkis and taxis run the 20 minute trip between Kara-Suu and Osh regularly. A *marshrutka* ride costs 10 som and a taxi 15-20.

**Karagoi

Karagoi is among the most beautiful places in all of Krygyzstan – a remote area of mountain peaks, rushing rivers, trees, flowers, and startlingly fresh air. A 2-3 day excursion here is time well spent. To arrange transporation, lodging in small but comfortable trailers, and food, contact Habib Djumabaev in Osh (Ul. Technicheskaya 20; Tel: 3222 76712; mobile: 0772 008740; 0772 278032; 0777 807831; Farhad 2113@mail.ru) Lodging plus three meals a day costs $40. Trekking, guides, translators and horses are available.

Uzgen

Pop: around 40,000

One would never guess that the dusty, bustling little town of Uzgen has existed since at least the second century BC, when it was mentioned in Chinese chronicles as the town of Yu. From 1000 to the 1200s, it was called Mavarannahr and served as a capital of the Karakhanid Dynasty, which ruled the area from 999 until Genghis Khan destroyed it in the 13th century.

Where to Sleep

There aren't any decent hotels in the area. If you must stay in Uzgen, ask around for homestay options.

Where to Eat

Café Navruz is in an unmarked building across from EcoBank, to the left of Ун Мука (red letters on a white building). When coming from Osh, take a left after the green building. Packed with locals at lunchtime, it serves up tasty *shashlik, samsi, pelmeni* and other simple but filling local dishes.

**Café Dosmat (on the road to Osh, a little bit out of town, past the bridge on the right hand side) is the best restaurant in Uzgen. Good beer. Salads 35-45 som, soups 25-26, mains 30-55. The *zhulen* is a nice chicken with cheese.

What to Do

The tourist highlight is the ancient **mausoleum and minaret, two relics of a past world standing in a grassy fenced in area and the oldest minaret and moque in southern Kyrgyzstan. The minaret was constructed during the Karakhanid government in the 9th to the 11th centuries. The middle mausoleum was built in the 11th century, the northern in the 12th and the southern in the 13th century. The red-brown clay mausoleums are marked by engravings and foliage on terracotta up to three centimeters deep, covering doorways, pillars, and walls. You can climb up the brick minaret to look over the sleepy section of town for 10 som (if it's locked, find the guard on the grounds). To get there, walk into town from the market. Keep an eye out for a silver Lenin statue on the right. The minaret is nearby.

A walk through the **central market is full of wonderful images. Go through the imposing blue and turquoise tiled pillars that mark the entrance and walk through the narrow aisles to find animal parts, crab apples, peaches, plums, tomatoes, cucumbers, fresh mountain honey, fat sold in vials as medicine, bags of flour, and sweet, yeasty smelling *lepushka*.

Transportation

A shared taxi to **Osh** costs 60 som per person. It takes 45-60 minutes on the newly improved road. On the way to Osh, keep an eye out for the people selling **fish** on the side of the road. It's some of the freshest, most delicious fish in the south. Expect to pay from 100 to 250 som and up for a string of fish.

Taxis to **Jalalabat** leave across from EkoBank. The price per passenger is 50 som.

To **Kurshab**, taxis leave from the central market. 15 som.

The Places of Kyrgyzstan – Uzgen

About two hours along a rutted road from Osh lies the ancient town of Uzgen, mentioned as far back as the second century BC. In early 2005, the roads leading to this historic town were filled with the signs of campaigning politicians, preparing for the February 27 elections. We heard the rumble of the Volgas headed to villages, seeking support. Dust rose from the road and seeped through the cracks in the window, filling our nostrils.

My driver, Malan, a middle-aged Uzbek, looked at the colorful and overwhelming displays, the caravans of cars toting politicians and their supporters, skeptically. He didn't plan to vote.

"They don't do anything for anybody," he said. "Last year a candidate came to my door. I asked what he would do to increase employment and he said he'd find people jobs. I told him, 'You don't have that ability and you shouldn't promise things you can't deliver.

Once you get in office you'll put a guard outside your door and tell him not to let in people like me because you don't have time.' He'll have a large salary, a private car and won't need to answer to anyone. He can practice corruption and will get a stomach out to here," he said, indicating a protruding belly.

Candidates posters were affixed to car windows and to shop fronts, their faces plastered across billboards, banners hanging over the roads, and caravans of Volgas "agitating," as the locals called campaigning. The faces of these politicians seemed to have replaced President Akaev's face, which a month earlier was everywhere. The mostly male candidates put mountains behind them, or showed their gentler sides through poses with family and children. But their oversized bodies and mean expressions spoke for themselves.

Mamat Orozbaev's billboard looked particularly mean. His serious face looked like a gangster peering out over the town.

"He's corrupt," Malan said, when I asked about him. "I know him."

Murat Malabaev looked nicer. His young face appeared on posters in small roadside villages. While driving in between snow-lined trees like still-life icicles, we went under a green banner reading "Let's vote for a good guy, Murat Malabaev."

"He'd be a good deputy," Malan said. "I hope he wins. He bought apartments for several people who didn't have homes. He also gathered pensioners and handed them each 100,000 som ($2,500)

> In contrast to countries where a politician's advantage comes from having enough wealth for self-promotion, in Kyrgyzstan, what makes a good deputy is having spent your own money to help people.

Kurshab

In Kurshab, between Osh and Uzgen, 24-hour watermelon stands operate from mid-August. There, through the fall, you can find the best watermelon in the area. The best place to eat is **Café Janybek-Ata**, near the central market. There are no hotels in Kurshab. If you are looking for a local translator or English-speaking guide, contact Nurgul Bektemirova (nurgul-ke@rambler.ru; Tel: 0772 02 15 77).

Aravan

Aravan is a small, agricultural town and a central spot for **caving** in the Fergana valley. The Aravan cave, made of limestone, is suitable for first-time spelunkers, but still challenging. To get there, go to Cherbak camp in Aravan. At the end, near the garage, you can find guides. Look for the *avtogarazh* sign. Upon leaving the area, look up the mountain on the left for a rock arch and a large Lenin silhouette.

Chili-Ustun is a famous and more difficult cave. Sergei Nasarov (Tel: 03222 25934; troglos-man@mail.ru). is a reliable guide for these caves and others.

Kara-Shoro National Park

A source of two locally famous natural springs, and a good place for both spectacular views of stars and hiking, Kara-Shoro national park is a bit difficult to reach, but worth a weekend trip for those who have the time. The director, Kabul-Jon, can be reached at 0502 414278 to confirm accommodations, but unfortunately, he is not very reliable. The park is located 70 kilometers (44 miles) past Uzgen, a little over two hours from **Mwirzake**. The entrance is 10 som/person, 40 per car.

There is a **mineral spring** on the way, about 30 minutes from Mwirzake, where cold, fresh water emerges from three tubes. Look for a tethering post across from a white picket fence and a white statue of two reindeer.

Where to Sleep

Zamira runs a tent-camp. A place in a large, basic tent costs 30 to 50 som. Her number in Osh is (03222) 64251. In the future, she plans to install showers and a banya.

Where to Eat

You can buy *koumiss* in the park. In summer, some local food might be available. It's best to bring some groceries.

Popan

The water reservoir at Popan, one hour south of Osh on the way to Nookat, is a picturesque place where you can fish. In summer, you might find yurts, Kyrgyz food and horses. Bring a blanket and a picnic.

Nookat

Pop: around 30,000

Nookat is a small, sleepy town, known for its tobacco, grain and apples. Living conditions are low but the people are especially honest and friendly. It's a place for the adventurous who want to see small town life. The ancient marketplace is a hightlight.

Where to Sleep

There are two hotels in town.

Where to Eat

Café Kyrgyzstan 2200 (ulitsa Kalenina, on the second floor, near Inexim bank) has marvelous giant *samsi* that are relatively low in fat as well as the usual assortment of Kyrgyz dishes. You can eat well for under a dollar.

What to Do

The **market** is bustling and a fun place to explore.

Just outside Nookat, in the Yangi Nookat (New Nookat) area is a tourist resort called **Sahoba**. The expansive, but basic complex includes a hotel, many cabins for eating and picnicking, space to rest and play, and mountains in the background for climbing. It is a holy place and pilgrims come to see the mosque and the rocks with ancient Arab inscriptions on them (in room to right upon entering mosque). Plenty of food and drinks can be purchased on-site and a simple hotel (mats on the floor) is available on the second floor of the two-story building (50 som/person/night; on the right as you enter). Compared to other natural sites in Kyrgyzstan, it's not worth a special trip to come here. But if you find yourself in the Nookat area, it's worth checking out, especially to see how the locals relax during summertime.

Transportation

**The road between Nookat and Aravan is a sparsely traveled rough stretch that used to be part of the Silk Road. It is dotted with caves and spectular views of mountains and rural life. If you have transportation and a free afternoon, it's a pleasant drive and a wonderful place for a picnic. Along the way, you'll see a river cut through a massive rock formation. The Soviets planned to close the rock gap in the late 1980s, backing up the river to form a reservoir. This would have flooded all the homes currently in the area. It was never pursued because the Soviets didn't manage to accomplish it before the fall of the Soviet Union.

The road from Osh to Nookat passes apple orchards, tobacco farms and the largest garbage pit in Osh.

Abshir-ata

**A tourist area on the Abshir-Sai river, in between Nookat and Kyzyl-Kia, this is a nice daytrip from either (about 2.5 hours each way) or a good place to spend a weekend. Water gushes out of a hole midway up the walls of a tall canyon, crashing down 12-15 meters (40-50 feet) into a bowl and splashing over a pile of rocks. The scenery is marvelous and unlike many Kyrgyz waterfalls, it doesn't require a long hike to get there. You can drive right up to the site, taking the road from Osh to Kyzyl-Kia, then bearing left at Kokjar. There is also a natural spring and nice hiking opportunities along the road through the canyon.

There is plenty of stream-side camping space available on the other side of the canyon. Or near the entrance is a simple tourist base which should operate year round.

Kyzyl-Kia

Pop: around 30,000

Kyzyl-Kia was formerly a very Russified town, with nine of the eleven schools Russian. It used to be home to factories as well as, reputedly, some work on bombs. After the end of the Soviet Union, employment opportunities crashed. In 1992 alone, 17,000 Russians left Kyzyl-Kia. It's now a small town with an active market. It suffers from a persistent lack of water and residents receive water only during scheduled times.

If you read Russian, you can learn more about Kyzyl-Kia at: http://kyzyl-kiya.com/

Where to Stay

Kyzyl-Kia has one Soviet era hotel in town, with rooms from 500 som. The standards are not very high. Five kilometers outside of town, in the village of Uchkorgon, is a nice hotel on the banks of the Isfairam river. Rooms start at 1000 som.

Where to Eat

Fill up on the best food in town at **Café Classic** (ul. Molodezhnaya 10, near AKB Bank). **Café Kyrgyzstan** (also on ul. Molodezhnaya) is also a favorite.

Café Marzhona (located to the right of Inexim Bank, near the market) serves the typical *plov* and beefsteaks. You can eat for 20 som.

In the village of Uchkorgon, five miles outside of town, you'll find a selection of *chaikhanas*, or teahouses serving traditional Uzbek food.

What to Do

Popular daytrips from Kyzyl-Kia include Abshir-Ata (see above) and the Pamir-Alay mountains. From the village of Pum you can take a three-day trek to Abshir-Ata.

Transportation

Kyzyl-Kia is 1.5 hours (90-100 kilometers or 56-62 miles) south of Osh, on a reasonably good road. A shared taxi starts at 150 som/person.

Other Services

AKB Kyrgyzstan and Inexim Bank have branches in Kyzyl-Kia.

Kojo-Kelen

Kojo-Kelen means "place where the holy man prays." About 300 years ago, a holy man lived near a grotto in this small village several hours south of Osh. He was buried just outside the grotto. As word of him passed through the generations, people came to the area to pray. Because of that, the village was founded 100 years ago.

Kojo-Kelen is a remote, rough-and-tumble village. There aren't many English-speakers there and even Russian is sparse. But it offers great hiking potential as well as the opportunity to witness traditional village life. This is a good destination for those who really want to get out there. There is a beautiful half day, 10 kilometer (six mile) hike that takes in the grotto in the cave, beautiful red cliffs and a waterfall. Several day hikes are also possible. From the mountain crossing, the Pamirs are visible.

On the way to Kojo-Kelen from Osh, you'll pass the Popan water reservoir, then travel through a 50 kilometer (31 mile) canyon to Kichi Kalai. At Bulak, a holy spring along the road, stop to wash your face there. It means you will return.

Upon arrival, contact Sabir (no telephone) to set up accommodation in a local house, a guide (500 som) or horses ($20). Look at CBT prices for a fair comparison and don't be afraid to barter if his prices are significantly higher. However, once you've reached Kojo-Kelen, the last village before nothingness, you don't have a lot of other options.

Batken

Batken is a difficult place to visit, due to the enclaves that separate it from the rest of Kyrgystan. To visit, you'll need to get an Uzbek visa, or to fly from Bishkek. **CBT** (Tel: (0312) 540069; 443331; reservation@cbtkyrgyzstan.kg, cbttours@mail.ru, a_rajiev@yahoo. com) currently has an office in Batken, but it may not remain open. Batken is attractive to climbers, who like to scale the famous 1-1.5 kilometer high vertical rocks.

Gulcha

Gulcha is the district center of Alay and is on the route between Kyrgyzstan and both the Tajikistan and China border crossing. There is an indoor hot spring pool that is worth a stop and a cheap hotel in town. **CBT** has a group in Gulcha (Tel: (0312) 540069; 443331; (03222) 20234; reservation@cbtkyrgyzstan.kg, cbttours@mail.ru, a_rajiev@yahoo.com). The Alay region is known as one of the places to have an authentic and uncommercialized shepherd's life experience.

Sary-Mogul

Continuing south from Gulcha, thorugh the Pamirs of the Alay valley, you'll reach **Sary-Mogul**, where CBT has a local group (Tel: (0312) 540069; 443331; reservation@cbtkyrgyzstan.kg, cbttours@mail.ru, a_rajiev@yahoo.com; B&B or yurt 400 som/night). Sary-Mogol is a good place for a view of the 7,134 meter (23,405 foot) **Peak Lenin**, or to start a climb. CBT also arranges **yurt camp** stays at Tulpar-Kol lake (3000 meters or 9,842 feet altitude), 25 kilometers (16 miles) from Sary-Mogol and one half day distance from the Peak Lenin base camps.

Crossing into China

If you want to head to China, you'll travel south of Osh through **Gulcha** (stop to visit the indoor hot spring pool; there is a cheap hotel in town) and **Sary-Tash** (plenty of homestays available, through CBT 550 som/night), where the road forks. You can hire a taxi in Sary-Tash to take you to the Irkeshtam pass. Travelers don't need any special persmission to cross at this location. Compared to the Torugart pass in Naryn region, **Irkeshtam** is less expensive, but more chaotic and time-consuming.

Crossing into Tajikistan

You can reach **Khujand** through Batken region. Crossing into **Jirgatol** is not recommended for safety reasons. The local authorities there are mostly former war commanders. If you go into the **Gorno-Badakhshan Automous Oblast (GBAO)** via **Sary-Tash** and the **Kizyl-Art Pass**, you'll need a special permit, issued by Tajik authorities. It is issued on a separate slip of paper, so it's possible to have it authorized in advance and sent by post before entering Tajikistan.

Crossing into Kazakhstan

As long as you have your visas in order, crossing from or into Kazakhstan is quick and painless. On the Kazakh side you have to get out and go through passport control. On the Kyrgyz side, if you are traveling by bus the guard might stamp your passport on the bus. Otherwise, you get out and they'll stamp it. You must walk a short distance across the border. If you are taking a vehicle across the border, you can leave your luggage in the vehicle.

To get to the border, you can take a *marshrutka* from the Dordoi and Alamadinski markets. Taxis and buses wait on either side of the border. Expect to pay about 8,000 tenge for a taxi from the border to Almaty (if shared, then divided among passengers). Or you can catch a bus or shared taxi all the way to Almaty from Bishkek and vice versa.

Almaty's clocks run one hour ahead of Bishkek.

Hotel Otrar (ul. Gogol 73; Tel: +7 3272 330-045; Fax: +7 3272 332-013) is a recommended and centrally located hotel in Almaty with 163 rooms. **Hotel Kazzhol** (ul. Gogolya 127/1) is also recommended as a moderate priced option. For those looking to splurge, the Hyatt Regency (ul. Academic Satpaev 29/6; Tel: 7 727 250 1234; Fax: 7 727 250 8888; almaty.regency@hyatt.com; http://almaty.regency. hyatt.com/hyatt/hotels/index.jsp) is top-of-the-line for top dollar. For additional hotels in Almaty see: http://www.kazakhstan.orexca.com/ hotels_almaty.shtml.

DiWang (75 Zhambyl Street, on the corner of Chaikovsky St.; Tel: 723810; closed Sunday) is an expensive, but high quality Chinese restaurant.

Just outside of Almaty is the famous **Medeo** ice rink. Previously a world-class speed-skating rink, it's now open for general skating until 11 p.m. It costs 200 tenge to skate and another 200 to park.

For skiers, there isn't much need to leave Kyrgyzstan, as no other Central Asian country can beat the combination of quality and value. However, if you find yourself in Kazakhstan, the best choice is **Chimbulak** (Tel: 7 (3272) 59-68-67; 58-19-99; Tel/fax: 7 (3272) 67-25-41; ChimbulakSR@mail.ru; one hour lift pass 1300 tenge, day pass 5000 tenge, ski rental available). Located 25 kilometers (16 miles) from Almaty, the 2220-3163 meter (7,280 to 10,370 foot) base has four chairlifts and a hotel that can accommodate 114.

Vorota Truk-Cy (278-1 Dostyk Av.; Almaty; Tel: 7 (3272) 640324, 541648, 607215; 607209; info@alpina.kz; www.alpina.kz), located at 2650 meters (8,694 feet), 1.5 km beyond Chimbulak, offers comfortable mountain accommodations. Prices range from 9000 economy (room 69) to 35000 for *lux*. An 8-person cottage is also available. Prices include breakfast and rise between December 20th and January 20th.

Andrei is a reliable driver who provides transport between **Almaty** and/or **Chimbulak** and **Bishkek** (Tel: 00787013979099).

Index

A

Abdurahmanov, Zhupov 60
Abshir-Ata 193
Abshir-ata 192
accommodation, Bosteri 79
Accommodations
  Talas 134
accommodations
  Bokonbaevo 109
  Cholpon-Ata 78
  Jalalabat 150
  Jeti-Oguz 101
  Karakol 92
  Kyzyl-Kia 192
  Naryn 122
  Osh 164
  Son-Kul 119
  Tamga 105
  Tyup 90
  Uzgen 186
accommodations, Balikchy 75
accommodations, Bishkek 24
accommodations, Lake Issyk-Kul 85
accommodations, Tamchy 76
Aerobics 53
aerobics 52, 53, 178
Afghanistan 4, 18, 150
Aimatov, Chingis 143
airport, transportation 8, 9, 24, 27, 46,
      48, 105, 177, 178
Airports 9, 25
Air travel 8
air travel 8, 9, 48, 55, 99, 152, 177
Aitmatov, Chingis 19, 21, 60, 142
Aitmatov, Turukul 60
Ak-Suu 100
Ak-Suu Region 91
Ak-Terek 104
Akayev, Askar 4, 5
Akmatbayev, Rysbek 83

Akmatbayev, T. 112
Ala-Archa 66, 67, 68
Alay 55, 193, 195
Ala Bel Pass 72
Alemeddin 67
Alexander the Great 162
Almaty 8, 9, 11, 46, 47, 196, 197
Altai 4
alterations 51
Ananyev, Nikolai 84
Ananyevo 84, 85
Arabic language 52
Aral Sea 2
Aravan 189, 191
archeology 74
Arkit 148
Arsalanbob 18, 55, 157, 158, 159
art 35, 40, 41, 51, 176
artists 39, 40
Astana 47
At-Bashy 126
At-Bashy mountains
  At-Bashy 127
Ata-Beyit 60
ATMs 57, 179
auto safari 55

B

Baazar Kurgon 159
Babak Baitir 112
Babushka Adoption 54
Baitik Batir 66
Bakiyev, Kurmanbek 5, 162, 176
Balikchy 10, 47, 75, 77, 79, 88, 112,
      113, 116, 117
Barskoon 103, 104, 105
Batken 55, 194, 196
Bazaar Korgon 156
Belasagun 70
Besh-Tash national park 140
Besh Tash National Park 141

bicycling 46, 53, 70
biking 53, 55, 56, 68, 75, 95, 99, 102, 105, 116, 118, 142
birth 16, 140
Bishkek 4, 8, 9, 10, 11, 12, 13, 19, 20, 21, 24, 25, 26, 27, 28, 29, 30, 31, 33, 34, 35, 40, 41, 42, 44, 45, 46, 47, 48, 49, 50, 51, 52, 53, 55, 58, 60, 61, 63, 64, 65, 66, 67, 72, 77, 79, 81, 92, 98, 102, 106, 110, 116, 123, 126, 134, 138, 139, 145, 146, 148, 156, 162, 177, 194, 196, 197
blogs 22
Bokonbaevo 11, 26, 46, 47, 52, 55, 108, 109, 110, 111
books 18, 19, 30, 39, 49, 51, 143
Boshkoi Batir Ozber-bai 66
Bosteri 74, 75, 79, 80, 81, 82, 86
bowling 45
bride stealing 21, 180
Bronze Age 162
Buddhism 62, 79
Burana Tower 70
buses 46

C

cakes 31, 51, 172
camera, repair 57
Caravan 148
cash advances 57
casinos 45
caves 63, 143, 174, 175, 180, 189, 193
cell phone 12, 51
Central Asia 18, 19, 20, 22, 37, 58, 116, 130, 134, 150, 176
chaikhana 193
Chaikhanas 170
Chili-Ustun cave 189
China 2, 4, 8, 10, 11, 124, 126, 127, 131, 150, 195
Chinese 4, 13, 52, 98, 126, 127, 131, 134, 184, 185
Chok-Tal 77

Cholpon-Ata 47, 48, 74, 78, 79, 81, 82, 98, 113
Cholpon Ata 77
Chonarik 66
Chong Ak-Suu Canyon 82
CHUI REGION 23
churchs 41, 53, 57, 92, 98
Cinema 40, 179
climbing 2, 56, 99
Communications 12
Community Based Tourism 18, 19, 27, 54, 55, 56, 76, 77, 90, 99, 109, 110, 116, 117, 119, 122, 123, 126, 127, 131, 134, 139, 141, 142, 150, 157, 158, 179, 194, 195
Cossack 84
Cultural Fund Sahna 41
Currency 10
currency exchange 99

D

Dancing 173
dancing 32, 34, 44, 52, 53
  belly dancing 52
Darhan 104
Dead Lake 79
Dead lake 81, 112
dead lake 112
Dentist 11
departure tax 9
dining, Bishkek 28
Drinking 173
drinking 44
drycleaners 56
Dungan 2, 98

E

election 5
elections 4, 188
Electricity 10
Embassies 11
Erkechtam pass 131
ethnicities 2

exchange, currency 9, 56, 57, 140,
    179

F

Fergana Valley 162, 163
festivals 18
Films 20
films 21
fitness 52, 53
Food 13
forel 75
Frunze 24, 25, 26, 40, 134, 139
Frunze, Mikhail 24, 40
funeral 17, 100

G

gas stations 12
Genghis Khan 127, 185
Golf 43
gorges
  Chon-Kyzyl-Suu 103
  Djuuka 103
Gorno-Badakhshan Automous Oblast
    (GBAO) 196
Great Game 19, 163
Grigorevka 82
Grigorevskoe ushele 82
Guidebooks 19
Gulcha 195

H

Health 11
Hertzen, Theodore 142
hiking 54, 55, 56, 58, 60, 61, 62, 63,
    64, 67, 98, 100, 102, 103, 105,
    123, 126, 127, 131, 147, 158,
    180, 189, 192, 193
holidays 12, 17, 96, 140, 153, 176
horseback riding 2, 16, 17, 43, 55, 56,
    74, 93, 104, 105, 106, 108, 110,
    118, 123, 126, 127, 131, 144,
    148, 158, 159
Horse games 16
horse games 35

hot springs 61
hunting
  with golden eagles 111
Hun period 140

I

Internet 13, 26, 31, 48, 81, 99, 139,
    156, 179
internet 126
Irkeshtam pass 178, 195
Issyk-Ata 46, 61, 62, 63
Issyk-Kul 10, 21, 46, 48, 55, 64, 65,
    74, 78, 80, 81, 83, 85, 93, 99,
    108, 109

J

jailoo 2, 17, 18, 43, 116, 117
Jalalabat 10, 18, 55, 72, 131, 148,
    150, 151, 152, 153, 159, 178,
    187
Jengish Chokosu 2
Jeti-Oguz 81, 99, 100, 101, 102, 103,
    105
Jirgatol 196

K

Kalmaks 145
Kalmyks 4
Kambarkan Folk Ensemble 20
Kant 46, 61
Kara-Koo 112
Kara-Kyrgyz Autonomous Oblast 4
Kara-Oi 74, 87
Kara-Shoro national park 189
Kara-Suu 18, 55, 177, 184, 185
Karabalta 60, 72
Karagai-Bulak 82, 85
Karagoi 185
Karakhanid Dynasty 185
Karakol 10, 47, 48, 55, 74, 79, 90, 92,
    93, 94, 95, 98, 99, 100, 102,
    103, 104, 108, 117
Karakul 72, 148
Karashar 113

Karatala 113
Kashgar 46, 122, 124, 162
Kashka-Suu 64, 98
Kazakhstan 8, 10, 11, 19, 27, 47, 103,
    118, 134, 138, 140, 144, 145,
    146, 196, 197
Kazarman 18, 55, 131
Kegeti 54, 64
Keltor 63
Kerben 55, 148, 151
Kereksizov, T.J. 79
Khaji-Say 106, 108, 109
Khan-Tengri 2
Khan's Grave 66
Khokand 4, 66, 175
Khorog 178
Khujand 196
Khurban-Eid 153
Kichi Ak-Suu canyon 83
Kirghiz Autonomous Soviet Socialist
    Republic 4
Kirovka 139, 143, 145
Kirovskaya Reservoir 143
Kirovskaya reservoir 146
Kizyl-Art Pass 196
Kochkor 18, 55, 116, 118, 119
Kojo-Kelen 193
Kok mainok canyon 63
Kok Sai 48, 144, 146
Koltso 67
Komsomol 82
Korkoram highway 126
Koshoi Korgon 126
Koumiss 14, 15
Kozhayar river 83
Krasnaya Rechka 61
Kurshab 189
Kuturgu 85
Kyrgyz 2, 4, 8, 10, 11, 12, 13, 14, 15,
    20, 22, 34, 40, 41, 52, 74, 78,
    117, 122, 131, 134, 136, 138,
    140, 144, 145, 152, 162, 164,
    173, 174, 175, 184, 196
Kyzyl-Adir 145
Kyzyl-Kia 178, 192, 193

Kyzyl-Oi 55
Kyzyl Suu 103

L

Lakes
  Chatyr-Kul 127, 128
  Holy 159
  Nulde 138
lakes, alpine 63, 74, 98
Lakes, Aragol 118
Lake Issyk-Kul 2, 74, 85, 94, 118
Languages 10
Language lessons 52
law firms 57
Legislative Assembly 5
Lenin 63, 187

M

Maimak 139, 144
Manas 8, 9, 11, 19, 24, 41, 48, 79,
    134, 140, 141, 142, 175
Manchus 4
Maps 19
maps 21, 24, 54, 123
Margilan 162
markets 51, 81, 98, 126, 138, 145,
    148, 156, 173, 176, 187
  Dordoi 37
marriage 15, 20
medical care
  Osh 180
military 50
mineral springs 10, 63, 65, 98, 99,
    100, 113, 150, 190, 194
money transfer 57
Mongol 4
Moscow 9, 47, 177
mosques 41, 98, 99, 143, 174, 176,
    191
mountains
  Boor-Albas 118
  Manas 144
  Moldo-Too 118
  Son-Kul 118

Suleiman 162, 163, 165, 174, 175
Teskey-Ala-Too 100
Tien-Shan 120
Museums 39
Music 20, 41
music 20, 29, 32, 33, 34, 41, 44, 45
Muslim 2, 4, 17, 79, 163
Mwirzake 190

N

Naryn 2, 10, 48, 55, 72, 115, 117,
   119, 122, 123, 124, 126, 127,
   131, 145, 195
Naryn River 2, 122
National Park 67, 68, 95, 98, 189
national parks 140
news 21, 22
newspapers 20
Nookat 190, 191, 192
Nooruz 58, 59, 60, 140
Norus 65, 66
Novokuznetsk 47
Novosibirsk 47, 177, 178

O

Oirats 4
Orlovka 65, 142
Ortuk 113
Oruu-Sai 65
OSCE 4
Osh 9, 10, 12, 13, 18, 48, 55, 72, 131,
   142, 148, 156, 162, 163, 164,
   168, 172, 173, 174, 175, 177,
   178, 179, 181, 184, 185, 187,
   189, 190, 191, 192, 194, 195
ostriches 21, 66, 67

P

Pamir Mountains 4, 164
passport photos 57
Peace Corps 11, 20, 22, 151, 172
Peak Lenin 2, 178, 180, 195
Peak Pobeda 2
People's Movement of Kyrgyzstan 5

petroglyphs 78, 108, 112, 131, 142,
   175
pharmacies 11
Pishpek 24
Popan 190, 194
post office 9, 12, 57, 78, 139, 178
protests 5
Przhevalsky, Nikolai 92, 95
Publications 18

R

rafting, whitewater 55, 56, 63, 180
RDS-Elet 144
religions 2
Research, services 57
resorts 65, 66, 74, 78, 80, 143
Chon-Kemin 55, 63
Chon-Kyzyl-Suu 103
Rivers
  Abshir-Sair 192
  Chon Kemin 63
  Chon-Kyzyl-Suu 103
  Chui 63
  Djili-Suu 103
  Djuuka 103
  Djuukuchak 103
  Isfairam 192
  Syr-Darya 162
Russia 8, 9, 11, 37, 47, 66, 103, 118,
   139, 162, 163, 178
Russian 2, 4, 9, 10, 13, 20, 22, 24, 32,
   52, 53, 70, 74, 84, 90, 92, 94,
   98, 111, 116, 140, 163
Russian Orthodox 2

S

Sadir-Ake 83
Safety 10
Saimaluu-Tash 18, 131
Sak peoples 78
Salons 49
salt caves 80, 117
Sanatoriums 63
sanatoriums 62, 63, 80, 81, 100, 101,

102, 103, 106, 117, 118, 144, 150

Sary-Chelek 27, 47, 72, 140, 147, 148

Sary-Mogul 55, 195

Sary-Tash 178, 196

Sasnovka 60

Sayan Mountains 4

Semenovskoye ushele 83

Semyonovka 83

Sheker 143, 144

Shepherd's Life 55, 56, 117, 126

Shoestring Canyon 75

Shopping 49, 51

shopping 50

shyrdak 17, 180

shyrdaks 2, 51, 110

Siberia 4, 47

Silk Road 18, 20, 124, 126, 162, 175, 191

Skiing 64

skiing 2, 46, 54, 55, 64, 66, 92, 95, 96, 99

Norus 46

Orusai 46, 66

Tugus-Bulak 46, 66

sleigh rides 159

Son-Kul 56, 75, 117, 118, 119, 120, 121, 123, 127

Souvenirs 51, 176

Soviet 4, 20, 24, 25, 26, 32, 35, 36, 40, 48, 58, 60, 61, 63, 80, 81, 84, 92, 96, 108, 135, 136, 138, 153, 162, 182, 191, 192

spas 25, 49, 52

St. Petersburg 177

Suluterek canyons 64

supermarkets 36, 173

Suusamyr valley 65, 72

swimming pools 26, 52, 53, 61, 65, 67, 80, 101, 102, 104, 195

Syr Darya 2

T

Tajikistan 8, 10, 11, 19, 162, 164, 195, 196

Talas 18, 47, 48, 55, 58, 72, 134, 135, 136, 137, 138, 139, 140, 141, 142, 143, 144, 146, 147

Tamchy 47, 55, 76, 88

Tamerlane 127

Tamga 55, 103, 104, 105, 106, 109, 110

Tash-Kumyr 72, 148

Tash-Rabat 123, 124, 126, 127, 128

Tasharik 141

Tashkent 2

telephone 57

Tengir-Too 20

tennis 42, 52, 53, 67, 175

Theater 24, 30, 32, 40, 52, 152, 173

Tibet 92, 134

Tien Shan 2, 4, 24, 55, 74, 99

Time 10

Toguz Bulak 65

toi 16, 138

tois 120, 121

Tokmok 34, 46, 69, 70

Toktogul reservoir 72

Ton 109

Ton Region 107

Ton region 108

Torugart pass 131, 195

Tosor 108

Traditions 15, 58, 153

Trains 47

Train Travel 9

Travel agencies 54

TSUM 36, 45, 51, 92, 99

Tsum 58

Tulip Revolution 17, 18, 21

Turkic 4, 70, 162

Turkish language 52

Turuk, river 60

Tuya-Asuu 65

Tuya-Asuu pass 72

Tuyug Issak-Ata canyon 63

Tuz 117, 118

Tyoplie Kluchi 67

Tyup 21, 48, 85, 90

U

Uchkorgon 192, 193
Uighur 2, 4
Uighur Kaganate 4
University of Central Asia 122
Urumqi 177
Usun peoples 78
Uzbek 2, 8, 10, 13, 14, 150, 154, 157,
    162, 176, 184, 194
Uzbekistan 2, 12, 19, 103, 118, 162,
    176, 184
Uzbeks 4, 162, 164
Uzgen 162, 178, 185, 186, 188, 189

V

Visas 8
Volunteer opportunities 41

W

walnuts 157
Water 10, 192
waterfalls 60, 61, 64, 67, 103, 104,
    105, 158, 193
Weather 10
weather 21
Web sites 21
wedding 43
Western Turkic khanate 70
White House 58, 124

Y

Yekaterinburg 47
yoga 52
yurts 17, 56, 67, 92, 93, 99, 101, 104,
    106, 108, 109, 111, 113, 116,
    120, 121, 122, 127, 128, 135,
    136, 137, 140, 175, 195